HYSTERIA

KATERINA BRYANT is a writer based in South Australia. Her work has appeared in *Griffith Review*, *The Lifted Brow*, *Island Magazine* and *Voiceworks*, amongst others. She has been shortlisted for the 2019 *The Lifted Brow* & RMIT non/fictionLab Prize for Experimental Writing, the 2018 Feminartsy Memoir Prize, and the 2016 Scribe Nonfiction Prize for Young Writers. She is currently a PhD candidate in Creative Writing at Flinders University. This is her first book.

To my family – Mathew, Mum and Dad

HYSTERIA

A MEMOIR OF ILLNESS, STRENGTH AND WOMEN'S STORIES THROUGHOUT HISTORY

KATERINA BRYANT

NEWSOUTH

A NewSouth book

Published by
NewSouth Publishing
University of New South Wales Press Ltd
University of New South Wales
Sydney NSW 2052
AUSTRALIA
newsouthpublishing.com

© Katerina Bryant 2020
First published 2020

10 9 8 7 6 5 4 3 2 1

ISBN: 9781742236773 (paperback)
         9781742244808 (ebook)
         9781742249308 (ePDF)

 A catalogue record for this book is available from the National Library of Australia

Design Josephine Pajor-Markus
Cover design Alissa Dinallo
Cover image Shutterstock/Freeda
Printer Griffin Press

All reasonable efforts were taken to obtain permission to use copyright material reproduced in this book, but in some cases copyright could not be traced. The author welcomes information in this regard.

This book is printed on paper using fibre supplied from plantation or sustainably managed forests.

CONTENTS

I.   EDITH   1

II.   MARY   41

III.   KATHARINA   99

IV.   BLANCHE   135

V.   KATERINA   160

EPILOGUE   187

FURTHER READING   195

ACKNOWLEDGMENTS   200

This book addresses the complex experience of living with mental illness. Please note that Lifeline operates a free, confidential twenty-four-hour online or telephone crisis support service with trained counsellors: www.lifeline.org.au, 13 11 14.

I.
EDITH

As I wheel the trolley into the supermarket, my partner, Mathew, already ahead of me picking out plums, my head begins to rush. I feel light, as if my bones have been taken out of me and I float along. Buoyant, I'm only flesh and blood. Mathew comes back, placing the crinkled bag in the trolley.

'You all right?'

I hadn't realised but since the rush of air filling my mind, I haven't moved. I'm standing still, frozen, a metre or so from the entrance. The trolley is empty bar the plums. I don't answer him. I'm caught where I'm standing. A stream of air pushes through my head; I haven't moved.

'Katie?'

A name only Mathew and my parents call me; I barely register his lips moving.

I move my eyes away from the silver lines of the trolley and up to him. It's hot today and the warm weather has made his hair curl up into its natural rings. I can see the thickness of his brows behind his glasses.

'Mmm', I mumble and try my best to nod. It comes out slow and measured, as if I'm trying to hold a conversation while reading.

Mathew takes the trolley from my hands and pushes forward to scoop up mushrooms. I follow him with slow short footsteps. My movements are a fraction of the speed of those around me. I'm immune to the urgency of Sunday late-afternoon shopping. Mathew places the mushrooms in the trolley and I can just smell their earthy scent. I look at their duotones, brown and white. They are small curls stacked up in a tray. They remind me of snails and somewhere inside me, I hear 'Snails in the supermarket!' and the hint of a laugh.

I follow Mathew, pinching the cotton of his t-shirt like a toddler would, moving towards the aisles. We walk past the fish, open-mouthed and eyes gaping, and I feel curious alarm. Did they always look like this? I look at the women and men behind the counter. They wear rubber aprons with brown leather straps. One is talking to a middle-aged customer with thick red-rimmed glasses.

The seafood line trickles out into our path and I struggle to move my body past the knot of people. I grip Mathew more tightly. He leads me away, pulling me into the safety of the aisles. I stand by the trolley as he runs up and down filling it with our staples: tofu and pasta, canned tomatoes and cheap soy milk. I can feel his annoyance. I have left this all to him. I will myself to move, walking down the aisle and loosely pulling the trolley beside me. I make it to the cracker section. *What do we need again?* My eyes cannot gloss over the brands as they usually do. They fixate on colourful packets and thick text.

It's beautiful. The bright mix of cardboard reminds me of driving up to Lobethal to see the Christmas lights with Yiayia. The cardboard shimmers under the gleam of fluorescent lights.

When we reach the checkout, I start to become myself again. As I come to, I can hear the music. Christmas carols playing in heavy loops. I ask Mathew, 'Have they always been playing?' He looks at me, confounded. He continues stacking the conveyor belt.

I pay and carry three out of the five bags back to the car: an act of penance. When we settle into the warmth of the car, I begin to speak. Short choppy sentences come out.

'I'm sorry. I don't know. What happened. It was. Too much.'

My spindly hands grip my knees. Mathew reaches out to them. I notice the line of hair on his forearm creeping up to his hands.

'It's okay', he says. 'Let's go home.'

This is just the beginning; I think this is what it's like to go mad.

*

'Illness', Susan Sontag writes in the opening pages of *Illness as Metaphor*, 'is the night-side of life ... Everyone who is born holds a dual citizenship, in the kingdom of the well and in the kingdom of the sick'. Running my experience of childhood through my mind, I'm not sure I've ever lived in the kingdom of the well. Compulsions laced the daily drives to school which arched around the city from Lower Mitcham to North Adelaide. My compulsive counting would distract me from the aggressively cheerful 1960s British pop Dad would play over and over.

But this feels like something stronger. Like a cloak taking me out of the world, at first small gaps and then swallowing hours in gulps. In the beginning, I did not recognise my own street, a leafy lane in Adelaide's CBD. Not only was I taken outside of myself, but outside of my home too. The Penguin-crime paperback-green of my fence was not mine. My hands and forearms did not resemble my own, either. I would drift in and out of living with no sense of place, or self, to tie me down.

I wrote this off as an almost-dream. It always happened while I was alone and so I doubted that it would stick. Until, that is, it all became much worse.

*

I try to read my way to an answer. That's always been my way; reading can solve the confusion of the world around me – even if it's Googling ambiguous movie endings. Mum is the same. Two months before I'd planned to visit South America, she forwarded me articles by the World Health Organization and refereed medical journals on the ebola outbreak, which was just beginning. We didn't talk about it

4

explicitly but after reading through the pages of symptoms, I chose to delay my trip.

I try to find a solution that will flood in as my experiences of unreality have, promising a sense of closure. In my obsessive reading, I find the work of psychoanalyst Edith Jacobson. While she is one of many Freudians I encounter, her first-person accounts of living closely with women who share my experience – depersonalisation – mark her out.

Edith was born in 1897 in Chojnów, Poland – known as 'Haynau' in German. I look up this small town by the Skora river with grand buildings topped by pointed orange roofs and try to imagine her there. I learn that Edith's family were a great influence on her. Her father, Jacques, was a kindly man. A GP, having previously been a military doctor in the First World War. Her older brother, Erich, was a paediatrician and Edith felt that this, too, was her path until she was drawn by circumstance to psychoanalysis.

It was in Munich in 1923, studying for her doctorate, where Edith first saw patients undergoing psychoanalysis. Working with Gustav Heyer on internal medicine at a local hospital, she witnessed first-hand his interest in gastrointestinal motility and how hypnosis influenced psychosomatic illness. Heyer was a Jungian, but one who Carl Jung later denounced for his involvement in the Nazi party. I imagine, although Edith's love of psychiatry stemmed from their relationship, that she too would have denounced Heyer without a second thought.

After Munich, in 1925 Edith travelled to attend the Berlin Psychoanalytic Institute. This would be where she learnt, practised and taught – her home – for her remaining time in Germany. I think of her entering the building for the first time, walking its halls and running her fingers along the thick wooden tables. I wonder if she felt it was a safe place, or if she sensed the threat that would come. Later, the institute's non-Jewish members would accuse her of putting it at risk.

It was while Edith was here, during the next four years of her study, that psychiatrist Arthur Kronfeld, who was sceptical about psychoanalysis, wrote to Edith's father to ask him to convince Edith to stop training. Kronfeld must not have known Edith well, as Jacques wrote in reply, '[my children are] quite used to being allowed to have an opinion of their own'. Jacques supported her despite calling her student fees the 'giant snake'. However, he died before Edith finished her studies in 1929. Edith left psychoanalysis, becoming a physician once again, to run her father's practice and care for the people in her hometown until she could sell the business and resume her life in Berlin.

After completing her training, Edith was drawn to child analysis and development. It was 1930 and her practice grew quickly, from children to adults from all spheres of society, especially working-class patients. Throughout her life, Edith kept her rate low so that psychoanalysis was available to everyone.

In the following years, Edith became increasingly interested in politics, especially given that she was a Jewish woman. Later she wrote, 'All I was interested in was science … But then, in the late twenties, Hitler turned up!

And acquired increasing power from the masses. Here was danger, I felt.' Edith, alongside other Berlin analysts, founded a small leftist movement within the International Psychoanalytical Association which hoped to combine psychoanalysis with Marxist principles.

Hitler came to power in 1933 and many of her peers, also Jewish leftists, left Berlin. Edith stayed. She wanted to be with her family; it's not clear whether this meant just her mother and brother, or included the men and women who pursued psychoanalysis endlessly, much as she did.

Edith continued her work with the Berlin Psychoanalytic Institute, but now her courses were not written in the 'official' program. She established a discussion group that was much like the previous faction meetings, where she wished to further the thought of German Freudian psychoanalysts. According to analyst Werner Kemper, here, Edith was 'the leading head – but also the heart'.

Edith continued teaching and secretly treated patients in the leftist resistance organisation *Neu Beginnen* (New Beginnings). She wrote that, 'What I did was accept two persons of this group who were highly intelligent but emotionally unstable into treatment.' I like to think that if I had been sick in her lifetime, I would've fallen into this group too. Some claimed that Edith was a member of *Neu Beginnen*; others viewed her as a therapist who also allowed use of her apartment for meetings. But in September 1935, the arrest of *Neu Beginnen* members led to difficulty for Edith. Her contact details were found in the home of a patient, Liesl Paxmann, an economics and philosophy student as well as a courier for *Neu Beginnen*.

In October, Edith was arrested. Despite her colleagues' and family's efforts to raise money for a lawyer, and the absence of evidence, she was indicted. Liesl had fled on her advice but came back to Germany on false information, where she was captured by the Gestapo, in whose custody she died. German philosopher Theodor W Adorno later said of Liesl's death, that 'it is not even known whether she killed herself … or whether she was murdered'.

Edith herself had escaped briefly to Denmark before her arrest but, as an acquaintance said, she had 'come back because she had not been able to stand it away from Berlin … and had anyway assumed that there wasn't really much she could be charged with'.

But, of course, she was wrong. As a young Jewish woman and Marxist she was a target, and when she refused to speak about a patient's circumstances, the Gestapo were, in her own words, 'very furious'. In 1936, she was sentenced to serve two and a quarter years in Jauer Women's Prison. Photos of Jauer are hard to find but there are records of other, similar women's prisons. They look like cold dark bunkers and have heavy tables bolted to the ground, where prisoners were lashed. I read of a woman who was kept in solitary confinement in Jauer for two and a half years. Another woman came to Auschwitz from Jauer and was reunited with her sister, who said she was in 'a terrible physical state'. I cannot comprehend what a place must have been like for a woman in Auschwitz to think it made her sister terribly ill.

In prison, Edith did not stop. Her life had halted in profound ways but she continued to work, writing papers and presentations. Another prisoner said that, 'Her incorruptible impartiality and strong will to live did not allow her to capitulate even in an apparently hopeless situation.' While she had written previously on the ego, Edith was now writing about the impact of incarceration on the ego: a key aspect of this was the depersonalisation prisoners around her were experiencing.

In prison, a place that by happenstance was near her hometown of Haynau, Edith fell ill with a reactive thyroid condition and diabetes. Her life was in danger, the prison doctor decided after taking an interest in Edith and talking with a colleague from Haynau, and so she was hospitalised in Leipzig. Edith was lucky as this was a time, according to her own understanding of politics, that the Nazi regime did not want prisoner deaths. If Edith recovered, she would return to prison. By chance, her older brother was working in the hospital in Leipzig. The resistance, along with friends of her brother, planned an escape. Edith was granted a consultation with a doctor in Berlin, where she left a suicide note to evade the Gestapo. She then travelled to Munich, received a passport belonging to an analyst friend, then escaped to Czechoslovakia with a pianist friend. In Prague, Edith underwent surgery and once she'd recovered, emigrated to New York. In preparation for her new life, she changed her name from Jacobssohn to Jacobson. It was there she built a ground-breaking career in psychoanalysis and lived well for forty years. She continued to live her life as a child-free, unmarried woman. All the while, diligently writing.

Edith's life is perhaps best thought of in her own words, taken from her paper on incarceration and depersonalisation. From her time in prison, she learnt that in some cases 'strong and intelligent women with a capacity for sublimation' may find, in being incarcerated, that they undergo a 'truly constructive development' where 'a new, mature structure and integration of the personality' occurs.

I realise, caught in Edith's world, that reading her life – full of successes and near-misses – is a kind of escape. I realise this especially after I find a photo of her. Edith's hair is pushed back from her face, coarse and sitting upright like my own. Her eyes and thick browline take over her face; hard work hinted at in small creases around her eyes. It's a simple photo, black and white. It is tempting for me to call it plain but there's this odd feeling, as I look at it, that beneath there is something extraordinary.

*

It takes a while for me to come to terms with what could be happening. It is so unknown: walls shifting and the faces of the people I love most becoming unrecognisable. I go to a doctor, then at her recommendation, a psychiatrist. I haven't been to a psychiatrist before, only a psychologist years ago who, as I was leaving, rushed to ask whether I was suicidal, in the same tone you might ask your partner to pick up bananas as they race out the door on their way to work. After that, I didn't return.

At the psychiatrist's office, I wonder if her face will be like Edith's, the woman I have read about in such detail. Will she possess serious eyes and a hint of a smile? Or is my imagining out of touch with the modern era, where psychoanalysis lives at the borders?

After walking through the long thin corridor, I find that the psychiatrist is dressed well and has soft, dark eyes. She's more sympathetic-looking than the photo of Edith I found and I realise I'm mirroring her movements. I've dressed well, too. Make-up, my nicest clothes. I'm scared that she'll see my madness in the darkness under my eyes, the unruly waves of my hair. They say hygiene can be one factor in showing that things are not all right, so I cover myself in a cloak of cleanliness. I take to wearing my chunky reading glasses, hoping they'll obscure the sickness held in my face.

As the psychiatrist notes my symptoms on a yellow legal pad, taking my family history, she mentions that my experience of unreality is something known as depersonalisation. It's the first time I hear the term applied to me and I fixate on it, that there is a name for this thing. If it has a name, I figure, then I am not alone. I can find a way out.

*

The term 'depersonalisation' originated in a journal entry by Swiss poet and philosopher Henri Frédéric Amiel. The entry was first published posthumously in 1884. He says:

And now I find myself regarding existence as
though beyond the tomb, from another world.
All is strange to me; I am, as it were, outside my
own body and individuality; I am depersonalised,
detached, cut adrift. Is this madness? No. Madness
means the impossibility of recovering one's normal
balance after the mind has thus played truant
among alien forms of being, and followed Dante
to invisible worlds. Madness means incapacity for
self-judgement and self-control. Whereas it seems
to me that my mental transformations are but
philosophical experiences.

Less than a hundred years later in 1952, it was written
into the first *Diagnostic and Statistical Manual of Mental
Disorders* (DSM), published by the American Psychiatric Association. Depersonalisation, here, is listed under a
heading of 'Dissociative reaction' and thought to be a part
of the medical definition of 'hysteria':

000-x02 Dissociative reaction

This reaction represents a type of gross personality
disorganization, the basis of which is a neurotic
disturbance, although the diffuse dissociation seen in
some cases may occasionally appear psychotic. The
personality disorganization may result in aimless
running or 'freezing'. The repressed impulse giving
rise to the anxiety may be discharged by, or deflected

into, various symptomatic expressions, such as
depersonalization, dissociated personality, stupor,
fugue, amnesia, dream state, somnambulism, etc ...
Formerly, this reaction has been classified as a type of
'conversion hysteria'.

But sixteen years later, with the publication of the DSM-II, the manual endorsed a position that the 'distinction between conversion and dissociative reactions should be preserved' and placed dissociation and 'conversion hysteria' as separate 'neuroses'. As the DSMs continued to be published, dissociation and 'hysteria' were more and more disentangled with each edition.

But despite the fluctuating definitions in the DSM, Amiel was right in that both philosophical contemplations of existence and depersonalisation are somewhat common. Psychiatrist Daphne Simeon and writer Jeffrey Abugel state that chronic depersonalisation is 'one of the most frequently misdiagnosed or underdiagnosed conditions in modern psychiatry'. Depersonalisation is the most common psychiatric symptom after anxiety and depression; the DSM-IV states that about half of all adults will experience an episode at some point in their lives.

Yet it is not often spoken of. Psychiatrist Aaron Kraser, talking to the *New Yorker* about dissociative fugue in 2018, said that 'There is an ineffable quality to dissociative cases. They challenge a conventional understanding of reality.' He continued: 'I think as a field we have not done our due diligence, in part because the phenomenon is so frightening. It's terrifying to think that we are all vulnerable to a lapse in selfhood.'

Almost 150 years ago, the term 'depersonalisation' was born with Amiel but dissociation and what comes with it still feels as foreign 'as though beyond the tomb, from another world'.

*

It was Edith's life in prison with other women where she learnt first-hand about depersonalisation, something her previous patients had never lived with. Edith found that given the right circumstances, depersonalisation is common. It was in prison that she wrote about the women she saw, in a paper that was later published. Her career to date had focused on the development of children; her writing here took a markedly different direction. She wrote, in a speech to be given at the New York Psychoanalytic Society & Institute in 1958:

> To my surprise I found that during the first weeks
> or months of arrest, many of these rather normal
> individuals developed states of depersonalization,
> evidently in response to their traumatic experiences.

Reading this, the word *normal* stings. As if the average person, with an absence of trauma and experiencing depersonalisation, is beyond reproach. I try not to dwell; my imagined Edith whispers that I might be projecting.

Shaping her words into something she didn't mean.

Edith held a number of interesting ideas on depersonalisation, one of which is her belief that the condition stems from a narcissistic conflict of identity. She writes, 'I noticed … a transparent connection of such states [depersonalisation] with the universal reaction of prisoners to the narcissistic blow inflicted by their arrest: the feeling that "this could not possibly have happened to *them*"'. To experience depersonalisation is to feel a split between the self and body. It is understandable that the trauma of arrest could bring this about in prisoners. Yet while it is enthralling to be reading more about the illness that is increasingly defining me, reading her study leaves me disappointed.

Why am I experiencing depersonalisation without trauma? What could be so intrinsically wrong with me that I mimic the detachment of prisoners? I begin to look harder for answers.

*

Before, I saw myself sharing mental health struggles with the rest of the population but now I'm not sure where I sit. My parents and I have this joke we like to repeat. Taken from the 2001 film *Rat Race*, Whoopi Goldberg's character contacts her daughter after years of estrangement, on the advice of her psychic. She says, 'She said you were lonely … and you were worried about money and you had trouble sleeping.' Her voice is soft as she speaks about her daughter's problems. Her daughter replies, 'Who the hell isn't?'

That's our joke. Who the hell doesn't have trouble sleeping, feel down and have the odd panic attack? One in five people experience a mental illness each year in Australia. Almost 50 per cent of Australians will experience a mental illness at some point in their lifetime. While I had racked up a considerable number of diagnoses (social anxiety, generalised anxiety, depression, obsessive-compulsive disorder), I felt within the realm of normal. At least, I was passing for normal. My illness was invisible; I had learnt to hide the compulsive behaviours and depressive episodes.

Now, that feels so far away. I can't trust my own vision. When I'm having an episode, I'm gone. Mathew sits with me and when he sees my eyes brighten up, he says, 'You're back.' I'm taking time out of my own body, as if my skin were something I needed a rest from.

I have episode after episode on the street. I see people looking at me strangely. The dazed, dead look in my eye catches them off-guard and they stare openly as I shuffle home. Once, I crossed a street at the traffic lights absent-mindedly. I was slow to cross – my hands straight at my sides to steady my body as I shuffled – and the green person ticked over to red. A driver beeped at me, loud and sustained, as they drove forward. I paid no notice as I shuffled on. The horn felt like it was coming from far away.

Another time, I'm walking home. It's a humid day and my feet have swelled in a pair of loafers my parents brought back for me from their trip to Italy. I remember video-chatting with them on their trip and Mum angling her tablet out the window so I could see their view. Now, the loafers rub as I walk the twenty minutes home. Five minutes after I hug a friend goodbye at the cinema, I'm having an episode. The hot pain at the back of my heel goes away and my body buzzes with lightness. As I walk home, I run my hands along the bark of thick bottlebrush trees. They scratch at my palms but I barely feel them.

I feel as though I'm in a parallel world, where I cannot think and everything I touch doesn't touch me back. I look at my feet, where the pain used to be. There is blood running down my heel. I hadn't noticed it. Usually, looking at blood, I would feel sick. I become nauseous looking at a paper cut but now I feel nothing. I keep walking.

I'm vaguely aware that as I walk, people are looking at me. Their eyes are fixed as I concentrate on moving my feet forward, staying on the footpath and avoiding the road. I think I see a parent loop their hand around a child's shoulder as I near, but that might be my mind colouring past memories. Three. Two. One block away from home.

When I open the door, I see Mathew on the couch. He is hunched over himself, eyes puffy; a small part of me far away knows he's just woken up. I stand in the doorway, still tingling from being outside.

'Katie?' He's instantly attentive.

I don't answer. I don't have the voice to speak to him. A second passes; he looks at me and my stare fixes on the shining yellow floorboards at his feet.

'Katie? Are you having an episode?'

My face crumples and I start sobbing. Thick tears

stream out of me and in the distance, I can hear the low coughs and splutters of myself breathing.

Mathew stands, taking my hands into his and guiding me onto the couch. I lie down and my backpack is still hooked around my shoulders. I can feel the curved edges of my drink bottle pushing through the leather and into my spine. I'm lying flat, stiff and straight. The tears keep coming and run sideways, soaking into the loose folds of my top. Beneath the tears, I feel numb. I am not myself; I am not anyone, yet I cry and cry at what I have become.

Mathew places my feet in his lap and removes my shoes. I feel him do this, but cannot see him. My neck is frozen stiff. I can't move and so I look up straight at where ceiling meets wall. They don't shift or grow. The walls are static and for that, I'm grateful.

As minutes pass – is it minutes? or seconds? – my tears start to slow. Mathew is rubbing my feet, stroking them from the tips of my toes to my ankles. I come back to him, as though I'm waking up after a deep sleep.

'I'm here.'

He puts my feet down and jumps up off the couch. This has become our normal. He moves as quickly out of the episodes as I do, ready to return to our lives. He looks at me, worry lifting. 'Shall we make dinner?'

*

After seeing the psychiatrist, I read more about depersonalisation. I spend hours each day reading through psychiatry books and Googling phrases ('depersonalisation unreal', 'alien unreal psychology') hoping that knowledge might unravel my episodes.

I start to believe that since my experience is ongoing, the answer must be depersonalisation disorder – a diagnosis that my psychiatrist did not give outright but I convince myself it fits. As it continues, episodes dragging across months, I think this must be it.

I learn that theories have changed since Edith Jacobson spent her days in a Nazi prison. Chronic experiences of depersonalisation are thought of as Depersonalisation Disorder (DPD) and there are three criteria for a diagnosis:

1. Persistent or recurrent episodes of feelings of detachment or estrangement.
2. Sensations of feeling like an automaton, living in a dream or a film, or as though you are an outside observer of your own life.
3. Symptoms are severe and ongoing so to cause distress and/or impairment in functioning.

I tick these boxes so completely that I feel a sense of relief. Madness, for me at least, has a diagnostic framework. And while most DPD sufferers experience the disorder chronically – all day, every day they feel as though they are not real – an episodic experience of depersonalisation is not uncommon. A third of sufferers, perhaps like me, experience episodes ranging in length from minutes to months.

Austrian psychiatrist Paul Schilder writes that, 'the

present is a concept which has meaning only in relation to experiencing personalities. The inanimate has no past, present or future ... Cases of depersonalization, whose total experience is splintered, all have an altered perception of time. In extreme cases, time seems to them to be at a standstill, or the present seems to be like the distant past.' 'Splintered' is an apt if depressing way to explain what it means to walk through the world without a sense of self. I have no sense of past in an episode or any ability to imagine a future where I am not this way; I am caught in a disintegrating present.

My favourite description of depersonalisation is by Ernest Hemingway, who might not have known it by this name. He wrote of a moment on the battlefield where he felt 'my soul or something coming right out of my body, like you'd pull a silk handkerchief out of a pocket by one corner'. The description makes me think of the quick swoop the episodes take and how quickly I am no longer myself. Hemingway continues, writing that his soul 'flowed around and then came back and went in again'. As quickly as you feel as though you are leaving yourself, as Hemingway shows, the return to normalcy can be as abrupt.

This sensation is called by many names, from an 'out-of-body experience' to 'astral projection', but 'depersonalisation' or 'derealisation' is what the diagnostic manuals call it. Knowing a name of an illness, reading it in a thick book, gives it substance.

*

It happens again. I'm sitting next to Mathew, taking in the smell of salt and pepper calamari and fried rice with thick eggy strands. I'm sitting across from a group of his friends. We see each other rarely, but still, they're family to him. Rae's baby, now eight weeks old, is sitting on the table. She's secure in her Todd's thick brown hands, lulled by his wide smile.

I don't notice it coming; it catches me by surprise. I look up from my small bowl of garlic-covered bok choy, and the veil has fallen. I see Laura speaking; her mouth makes the motions and I hear her but can't concentrate on the words. Behind her, the wall zooms out. As if this restaurant is a movie set, all cardboard and paint. It feels flat; the wall flexes and shrinks. It breathes. It feels more alive than I do.

I look at my hands and forearms to collect myself. I hope they will ground me, take me out of this. But they are not mine. The way the skin wrinkles around the joints of my fingers is unfamiliar. They are alien. I start to panic.

They can't know, they can't know, they can't know.

I'm frightened but my voice sounds steady and rhythmic as I think through these words. When I'm like this, I usually can't think anything but slow, woozy thoughts. Now, I'm caught up with a purpose. I can't have them knowing I'm sick. How would they feel having someone they love anchored to this?

I think of the baby. The moment I felt her weight in my arms. The hospital walls were orange-pink with an elaborate teal trim stamped along the ceiling, a remnant from the 80s. She was small but still so much bigger than the other newborns. I think of her heavy low cheeks and hair that stretched across her scalp. I've never felt the connection to babies some people have. I prefer children who can speak back to me, who draw and play games and like animals as much as I do. But with the baby, her body grows sleepy in my arms. She trusts me. It takes her a stretching five seconds to react after I tap her nose. I'm in love.

They can't know, they can't know, they can't know.

I stand up, shaky on my feet. My knees feel floaty, as if the lightness in my limbs means my body will stretch up and dust the ceiling. I walk to the bathroom, the wood of my clogs slapping the floorboards. I walk into a cubicle and sit, staring at the broad white wall. My elbows collapse into my knees. The wall glows under the fluorescent lighting. I keep staring, hoping for all this to fade away. The wall stretches out, growing, as if I've put a camera to my eye and flicked 'zoom'. It flexes, spreading slow then shrinking again. Writing this now, I remember the throb of the wall in *Nightmare on Elm Street* with its reaching hands. But while this experience was frightening, it was nothing like the film. Seeing the wall grow, my ability to be frightened was dulled into obscurity.

I walk out of the stall to wash my hands, watching the shapes and lines of my face as I do, lingering on the dark grey crescents under my eyes. It's not a face I know. To be honest, it doesn't look like a face at all. Just a mess of bones and skin.

As I walk back to the table – hearing my shoes in the

distance, clop clop clop – I see the restaurant lights flicker. *Someone should change the lights*, I think as I sit down. I don't make eye contact with anyone; I'm scared to be seen so I look into my bowl. With a dulled, scratched spoon, I scoop bits of rice and tofu into my mouth. I chew and it feels slow and monotonous. The food has no taste; it's all texture. Small grains of rice catch in my throat as I try to swallow. Mathew is talking to Laura and the voices are distant, like a flight call over the speakers in an airport. I continue to bring food to my mouth and chew, scared to be noticed. It's an excuse not to talk.

They can't know, they can't know, they can't know.

A waiter lifts up a plate and I test my voice. 'Thank you.' It's loud and clear but not my own. I'm sick of the sensation of chewing and swallowing; without taste, it's sickening. As the spoon lifts up to my mouth, I don't recognise my own hand. *You're not real*, a voice in my head echoes.

My eyes glance up to Laura. She sits across from me and the wall behind her is stretching out. I look to the side and Rae is holding the baby near a gold canvas. It's larger than she is and the two of them rock back and forth comfortably. The canvas shines against the restaurant lights and I hear Rae: 'There's a boy. He's holding a pear.' I look to Laura, but her face isn't hers. It's flat. There's no dimension there and I can't recognise it.

They can't know, they can't know, they can't know.

It's getting worse. I turn to Mathew. His face, too, is unrecognisable. I know it's him, at least intellectually, but

I don't feel it to be so. The voice in my head is loud. *You're an alien. You're not human. You're not here.*

I reach out to grab Mathew's hand.

He looks at me, frowning. Shifting his hand away slightly, confused I think. I never do this. We're not the type to be affectionate in front of others. I reach out again, gripping hard. His hand has no warmth. He usually runs hot, but now I can't feel him. I keep smiling and nodding, but my teeth are gripped tight. I shift my eyes around the room, back and forth. They hurt. I can feel my vision fixating on the tablecloth in front of me, an oil spot next to my glass, Laura's red handbag. I look for a moment then tear them away, only to fixate on the next item. The voice has quietened and Mathew's hand, still linked to mine, begins to warm.

They can't know, they can't know, they can't know.

I breathe out and the rest of the evening passes in a blur. As we walk out of the restaurant, I pause awkwardly as Rae manoeuvres the pram through the doorway. I look back at the table, now empty of dishes, and notice the lights are still.

They weren't flickering, after all.

*

Edith writes:

The dreadful change of surroundings, the restriction of normal everyday activity and the severing of all object relations mobilize the hostile instinctual powers from within. Unexpectedly struck, the ego of the prisoner has to face a fight on two fronts: Against the outside as well as against his own inside world.

*

In 2014, Daphne Simeon and Jeffrey Abugel wrote about depersonalisation in the first definitive book devoted to the subject. The book, *Feeling Unreal: Depersonalization Disorder and the Loss of the Self*, looks at the myriad ways a person experiencing either chronic or episodic depersonalisation may feel.

They write of a patient named Sarah:

Sarah, a 29-year-old graduate student from Long Island, New York, has dealt with depersonalization for most of her life. She explains the sensations to others in terms to which they can relate. 'Most people have played little games with their minds at one time or another,' she says, 'like staring in the mirror so long that you no longer recognize your face, or repeating the same word over and over until it no longer sounds familiar – it sounds like something you've never heard before.' These momentary impressions of strangeness that normal people can induce in themselves are quite similar to what Sarah feels much of the time, but cannot control, she says.

Sarah's description of the experience is telling. Her account is as much about the process of describing depersonalisation to those around her as about the experience itself. It is a pressure I too feel keenly. Throughout my reading, I am surprised by how much the same terms come up across varying cultures, countries, genders and life experiences. I read about feeling 'alien', like a 'robot', an 'automaton' or a character in a movie in which the person is watching themselves. I hear myself say these words to Mathew, Mum, Dad, my GP, my psychiatrist. It's a repetitive cycle of feeling as though one isn't quite human, and then relating this to those who are closest to you. Or rather, trying to relate it, as so often your audience can't know what it's like unless they too experience it.

Psychoanalyst Jacob Arlow explained the experience by comparing it to dreaming. Both dreaming and depersonalisation create an atmosphere of unreality and a skewed sense of self, in which one part of the self is an observer and the other is the one participating in life. Dreaming is an accessible portal through which the uninitiated can try to understand the frightening, surreal and detached experience of feeling like an automaton.

Sarah's account is also interesting in that she, too, shows that we are all able to touch the experience in the everyday through what she calls 'little games'. Apart from the perhaps universal experience of repeating a word over until my tongue becomes dry and it sounds senseless, I feel the impact of these 'games' during my work as a tutor. I mark essays by twelve-year-olds, writing about whether or not they should have homework, or Dickensian narratives about orphans overcoming impossible obstacles. Looking at the shape of their handwriting, words often look wrong or strange. Seeing it over and over again, I check the spelling on my phone. It's right, most of the time. But the shapes and repetition make the words in their clumsy loose letters look odd. Almost unreal.

But games cannot explain depersonalisation's sister experience: derealisation. The two, while they can be separate, are often connected. Derealisation can also manifest in the idea that you are looking at familiar objects for the first time. Say, for example, you play the piano; you sit down to practise as you do every day and feel as though your fingers have never before touched *this* piano. Intellectually, you might know that you play here every day but regardless, the smooth black and white keys look unfamiliar.

Simeon and Abugel write of one woman's derealisation and her experience of looking at objects as if she had never encountered them before:

'I sometimes feel like I'm from Mars,' says Cheryl, a 33-year-old fabric designer. 'Being human seems strange, bodily functions seem bizarre … My thoughts seem separate from my body. At times, the most common, familiar objects can seem foreign, as if I am looking at them for the first time. An American flag, for instance. It's instantly recognizable, and immediately means something to everyone. But if I look at it for more than a moment, I just see colors and shapes on a piece of cloth. It's as if I've forgotten ever seeing the flag before, even though I'm still aware of what my "normal" reaction should be.'

Cheryl's story is all too familiar to me. In the first days of being ill, the unreal, 'new' quality trees took on was alarming. It made me realise, as Cheryl does, the importance objects hold in making up the fabric of our identity. Without being grounded by the objects around us and their sense of reality, it is all too easy to lose one's sense of self and stability. French philosopher Jean-Paul Sartre writes of this very phenomenon in his novel *Nausea*. The protagonist, Antoine, finds himself in a park unable to name the nature before him:

> The roots of the chestnut tree were sunk in the ground just under my bench. I couldn't remember it was a root any more. The words had vanished, and with them the significance of things … I was sitting, stooping forward, head bowed, alone in front of this black, knotty mass, entirely beastly, which frightened me.

It's curious to me that both Sartre's character Antoine and I are caught on trees. Something about losing one's knowledge of trees is more alarming than not recognising an everyday item like a smartphone or a kitchen chair. Trees are alive. They came before humans did. For me to lose my sense of them – and Antoine their roots, which keep them alive and breathing – feels particularly tragic. It shows how far removed I have become from the world.

As Sartre shows in *Nausea*, depersonalisation does not live in textbooks alone but touches the world of fiction too. He writes of Antoine:

> I can't say I feel relieved or satisfied; just the opposite, I am crushed. Only my goal is reached: I know what I wanted to know; I have understood all that has happened to me since January. The Nausea has not left me and I don't believe it will leave me soon; but I no longer have to bear it, it is no longer an illness or a passing fit: it is I …

Antoine begins to assimilate himself with the depersonalisation so that he exists in a state of flux. Caught without an identity, he lives in a liminal space between life and death. This is what the French call, 'le coup de vide'. *The blow of the void.*

Antoine realises that he no longer has to 'bear' it, for the illness is him. So often, as for Antoine, depersonalisation is seen as something to be suffered through. It is frightening at times and can make a person feel disconnected from those closest to them. Like so many illnesses, it isolates you fully. Yet, as Simeon and Abugel found when interviewing a woman in her 40s, the experience is nuanced. It sits in a place of neither condemnation nor joy. They write:

Said one recovered depersonalized individual ...
'depersonalization changed my perspective forever,
in an existential way. But when I first experienced
it, all I wanted was a way out. It took me a long
time to realize that I wasn't going insane. I'll always
envy people who just live within the framework of
normalcy. Yet sometimes, I feel a little sorry for them,
especially when they're overly self-confident. They
think they know who they really are.'

Perhaps it takes being stripped down to nothing, losing all
sense of self, to find the joy in living. Feeling outside of
myself may allow me to connect better with who I am; that
is, when I feel present.

There's a line in the movie *Silver Linings Playbook*
where the character Pat, who experiences bipolar disorder,
says, 'Maybe we know something that you guys don't,
okay? Did you ever think about that?' I used to think it
was wishful thinking that my illness would give me greater
insight into the world. Sometimes pain is just pain, without
giving you anything back. But now I'm no longer
certain. To come out of depersonalisation is to feel connected
to yourself. It's hard to worry about the shape of
your nose or the ballooning of your belly when just recently
you were convinced you were an alien.

Perhaps to know the extent of your own resilience,
fully, is an experience to be cherished.

*

Edith spent some of her time in prison writing poetry, a habit that continued beyond incarceration into her life in America. Her poems are now buried – accessible but inaccessible in that administrative way – kept in boxes in the Library of Congress, Washington DC. I email them and wait for a reply, expecting nothing, and then thirty photographs of Edith's poetry are sent to me.

The pages are near-illegible, loose fountain pen script crossed out and rewritten. Most poems are written on yellowed sheets of paper, some with addresses scrawled in a different pen on the other side. It reminds me of Mum scribbling ideas on envelopes while she waited to pick me up from school, unable to talk until she had finished scrawling. A few of the pages have a letterhead. It's the one thing I can read, stamped in English above the German:

Edith Jacobson, M. D.
550 West 96th Street
New York 25. N. U.
Academy 2-4007

Through the photos, I can see the folds of the paper. Small rectangles as though Edith folded them up tightly and kept them in her pockets as you would a shopping list. The earliest poem was written on 31 October 1940; she'd spent two years in New York by then. The latest is 1952 and the rest remain undated. Only three of the thirty are typed, over which Edith has added a comma or a line break in her own hand. One of these, untitled, is in English:

The time, this wonder full of mystery,
Abiding now, escaping then our mind,
The time bewilders still our aims to find
Light in the darkness and our problems key.

But time creates the anniversary
To be a symbol, as we are inclined
To promise and fulfil, the kindest kind
To celebrate our dearest good: to be.

So be aware of the eternal truth
Which we are representing, we, the youth,
That where is love there always is the prime.

You shall grow young for ever, dear old boy,
With us, the youth, and thus you shall enjoy
The timeless happiness of living time.

I try not to project too much on to this, the only intimate message Edith has left that I can understand. 'The time bewilders still our aims to find/Light in the darkness and our problems key.' Is this about life in general or the war Edith just survived? 'Our dearest good: to be.' Is this surviving or living? I have her in front of me and yet I find I'm still grasping at her meaning.

*

I realise I've encountered the idea of depersonalisation before, during an evening at the beach. I go back again and again to this moment, two years before my illness began. It's as though by returning to these memories – to this moment where I learn one small part of what my future illness will look like – I can make myself remember more of what life was like before. Often, late at night, when the house is so dark I cannot see my outstretched hands, feeling along the shapes of the walls, I can convince myself that this memory is different. And perhaps, understanding depersonalisation better now, I can rewrite what has happened since.

It was Mathew's friend Kurt's birthday. Kurt's friends all wore dark cloaks with a hood that could be brought up to cover half their face. They looked odd in the beach setting. The dark drape of their clothes contrasted with the white and yellow of the sand. I assumed the robes were a tribute to the heavy metal they loved, but I never asked.

I remember sitting by Mathew near the shore and burying my feet. The cool wet of the sand relaxed my toes. My hands kept busy collecting layers of sand as I drew patterns by my feet. It was the first time I had met Kurt and I remember his height – well over six feet – and the cotton-candy effect of his long blond beard.

Kurt speaks quickly and is quick to laugh, making you feel welcome in his presence. I immediately understood why he and Mathew had been friends for so long. Kurt was open with us. He spoke of seeing a psychiatrist and how he had begun experiencing depersonalisation. He explained, standing, while Mathew and I sat on the sand, the damp crawling up into our clothes, that he was outside of himself. He didn't feel like a person. While he spoke, he looked Mathew straight in the eye. I wonder, now, if he was doing something I have come to do: watching carefully for a hint of fear in the person you're speaking to. Or alarm, something that rises to someone's face so quickly that they cannot help it. Occasionally, I will not look. I will be too scared to see, yet again, the judgment in another's eyes.

I remember what it was like to be on the other side of that conversation. I felt a mix of emotions as I listened to him. First, pity. *That is what it looks like to be ill*, I'd thought. His psychiatrist told him that it was okay, for now or forever, if he didn't hold down a full-time job. He needed help in a way I couldn't understand. Not then, anyway.

Hearing about depersonalisation for the first time, I also felt a touch of fear buried deep. If Kurt wasn't connected to himself, what did he feel towards others? What was he capable of doing? Writing this, I feel ashamed at my small-mindedness, and that when hearing about someone struggling with their mental health, I thought of myself.

I talk to Mathew about Kurt and his depersonalisation three years after that day at the beach. I recount my pity for Kurt and Mathew looks at me, an eyebrow raised.

'That's not what happened.'

I scan his face for the hint of a joke. 'What do you mean?'

'You don't remember? After we left, you said how men can often be forthcoming with mental illness while it's harder for women.'

I sigh a heavy rush of air.

'Fuck. That sounds exactly like something I would say.' Now I know more. It's not just gender, although that plays a part.

'When you're so ill, it's hard not to talk about it. To be forthcoming. Often, it'll spill out of me to people I wasn't sure I wanted to tell. It's just always cycling through my head.'

Mathew is listening intently and I suddenly feel a tiredness aching through my bones. I move towards him, nestling my chin into where neck meets shoulder. Stubble scratches my jaw and I feel the warmth of him.

*

I start to think Edith and I are the same. She was on the other side of the couch, yes. But we share so much. Edith, in an admission interview, when asked why she wanted to become an analyst, she answered, 'Because I have such a curiosity.'

Her father, before his life as a GP in Haynau, was a military doctor in the First World War. He was wounded in 1916 in this role and went on to experience what Edith later described as a 'severe depression', culminating in time living at a 'sanatorium'. Edith's later research on depression was inspired by her father; her talks at the New York Institute on the topic were said to be 'legendary'. Edith wrote of loving her father deeply, calling him 'an adorable person' and I see within – or maybe project on to – her actions not just curiosity, but an intense desire to help.

Before this illness, like Edith, I was curious about the world around me. Now I am obsessed with what lies beneath. I think of my brain, electricity pumping through as scattered and unreasoning as the world Edith found herself in.

*

Thoughts come in drips, slow and thumping. Punctuated by silence, not like the everyday rush of my mind thinking through shopping lists and what I've written that afternoon. I'm at my parents' house with Mathew. Suzie, our dog, has taken to ignoring my parents' dog, Ginnie, for the comfort of Dad's rough pats. We play bridge and I'm on Mum's team. I'm wearing clingy soft grey pants. Every half hour, Dad speaks into his Apple watch loudly, telling the feminine-voiced robot to set another timer for the sprinklers.

Mum and I sit across from one another, tallying our cards and scoping each other's bids.

Two hearts.

We win the contract. This round, I'm the dummy. I lay out my cards and Mum peers over at them. I start to feel myself spacing out. I stare at the glass of carbonated water, bubbles popping up one after another, across the table.

Mum holds out her cards and I see a row of thirteen dog faces reflected back to me. I had them printed up last Father's Day and chose a picture of Suzie that looks more melancholy printed on a pack of cards than it did on my computer screen. The cards are shuffled both upside down and right way up and the mix sends my mind into a blur. I breathe evenly as I straighten my own hand laid out on the table.

The fixed stare becomes too much.

'I'm going to make a tea', I mumble. I can hear that my speech is already affected. I walk as steadily as I can out of the room and down the hallway to the kitchen. I make myself go those five steps further to flick the kettle on. If they hear the kettle boiling, they won't be worried. It will buy me five or so minutes to wait for this to pass.

That's the last thought to run through my head for a while. I lie, face down, on the carpet outside the kitchen. The thick wool scratches my cheek. I know this from lying here before, but now, I can't feel the rough fibres of the wool sketch patterns in red across my cheeks. I only feel the hollow hum of numbness.

I am facing the kitchen. From where I lie, the white cupboards that touch the ceiling have a looming quality to them. They seem to stretch and flatten against the wall. I look at their gold knobs. The shadows beneath them flex and dizziness overcomes me. I close my eyes. The lids are heavy.

I can hear Mum in the other room. She's laughing and Dad says something. Maybe, 'No, I trumped it.' I can't follow what they're saying. They feel like snippets of a conversation wafting over from next door. But it's comforting hearing the recognisable shapes of their voices. They are far away but I know it's Mum, Dad and Mathew. I'd worried that a moment will come when I might not even know it's them.

The hand finishes. Mum's chair scraping back marks the end of the game. She walks out into the hallway. She is quiet. Why doesn't she call out to me, as usual? I feel her coming closer. I hear the crack of her sore knee as she sits, cross-legged, near my head. She places her hand, small and bony, in the crook of my neck and runs it down to my left shoulder. She repeats the action, stroking me gently.

I know it's her, but don't feel this to be true. In an episode, it's like reality fractures. There's what I know and what I feel. I know this is my mother's hand but it doesn't feel human. I can't feel the warmth of her touch. Her hand feels as though I am brushing against an object, not the woman who has cared for me for the entirety of my life.

Mum begins to speak, 'Breathe deep, love. Big, deep breaths'.

I tell her I can't.

'What was that?'

The carpet must have muffled my words. My lips are limp and my voice feels stuck.

'I can't.'

'Try.' Mum places her hand on my back, in the centre where my lungs meet. She breathes loudly – in and out, in and out – and it takes every bit of energy I have to do the same. I am so outside of myself, as if someone has folded up and tucked away my very essence, that breathing feels beside the point.

'Keep going, deep breaths.'

I hear my own breath. It's pathetic next to Mum's. Small wheezes where my chest barely moves. I go back to closing my eyes; the zoom and twist of the grey carpet is too much, bringing on dizziness.

Slowly, I come back into myself. I feel Mum's hand with all of its warmth. I push my body up, resting on my elbows and looking at Mum. Her hand sits on my shoulder, still.

'I feel better.'

Mum's face stays still. Her skin looks grey in the low light.

'Really', I assure her.

She doesn't move, but speaks now. 'You sure? Don't get up too quick.'

Her dog, Ginnie, walks up to us. Mum named her after Virginia Woolf and she's all legs and wet brown eyes. She flops beside us and I crawl over to her, burying my nose in the short blotches of brindle fur on her thighs. I inhale and she smells of dust and wood.

'I'm fine.' My hand is now rubbing Ginnie's pink belly, covered in brown dots as if flicked with paint. 'It's over now.'

Later that night, I lie next to Mum on the soft white cloud of her bed. It's a heatwave in Adelaide and Mathew, Suzie and I are sleeping at her house where there is air conditioning. Our dust-filled fan from Kmart hasn't been up to the task this summer. Suzie and Mathew sleep on the couch while I share a bed with Mum. Book in my lap, I ask if the episode scared her. She pauses, unsure how to answer the question.

'Be honest, Mum. It's okay.'

Her fingers flick up as if she were drumming them against a table.

'It ... was worse than I thought it would be.'

I reach out to hold her hand. I look at how small her wedding ring is on a finger much thinner than my own.

'Did it become real?'

'It was always *real*. It is just confronting to see your child like that. You were gone, in that moment.'

I sigh, my back molars tense against each other. I hate seeing the anxiety this creates in her, in Mathew.

'I know.' Her hands are weaving themselves together.

'We'll find an answer.'

That night, in the cool of Mum's room, I dream I am rebuilding myself. I am outside of myself, sculpting a new body out of bright bits of play-doh. I stand back to look up at my new, multi-coloured body; I am tall and look grand in the dark room of my dream.

Like Edith, I am strong. I have emerged as something far away from myself.

II.
MARY

Before my CT scan, I am sitting in my kitchen with Mum, and she reaches into her bag to give me her perfume. It smells rich and woody with notes of lime. I roll it across my wrists and collarbones, the thick oil of it sitting on top of my skin.

She's here to drive me to my appointment. She has asked me not to drive, as the episodes have become more frequent. It's best not to be on the road when I can't always be sure if I'm a human being. It feels like I'm giving up something big. Mum and Mathew begin to send text messages throughout the day asking how I am. I'd find this frustrating, but I don't trust myself either.

At the scan, I lie on a metal table covered in thick surgical sheets and place my head between two thin metal walls. My back feels rigid against the table and my hands naturally clasp together, tight across the round of my stomach.

'Lie as still as you can', the radiographer says. 'If you move it can blur the pictures.'

The bed slides up into a thick plastic loop. If I am Saturn, this is the ring around me, whirring and pumping with metallic purrs. From where I lie, small green lights dart around me, blurring into lines. I watch them spin and slow, then jerk in the other direction. The fluorescents catch the corner of my eye. Their bright green tinge makes my eyes blink in thick heavy movements.

I'm trying so hard not to move. A minute passes before I notice that the bones of my hands are now cutting into each other. I think of Dad and the year we didn't know what was wrong with him. The neurologist left it as a question mark and we were so relieved that he was better that we just let it go. Is that what will happen here? I remember being in year seven and a girl saying, 'Dad is in the hospital today.' I was relieved for it to be normal. 'Mine is too,' I said. It was only when she began talking about his surgeries that I realised her dad was a doctor and it was only mine who was sick.

The whirring slows and eventually stops. I try to get up but am too dizzy. The radiologist puts her hand on my back as I sit up and I look down at the rainbow tassels on her loafers. She is young. I think of how my friend's little sister is already making more money than a writer could imagine, taking scans of people's knees, hips and heads. I'm relieved I have a healthcare card so they can bulk-bill the scan.

When I'm steady, Mum and I walk back to the waiting room. We walk past a worn stuffed rooster placed head-first in a mock CT scan. She laughs while I stay quiet. My mind is with the whirring green lights and what the scans will show.

After a minute, the radiologist walks into the waiting room to pass me a huge envelope. I walk out into the car park and pull out the scans as soon as I can, holding the thick grey sheet to the afternoon sunlight.

A CT scan effectively shows a three-dimensional view of the brain. Slice by slice. When the psychiatrist fumbled to slip on her patent wedged heels to rush to the phone and make an appointment for a scan, I recognised her urgency. I knew what she was looking for. I didn't have to understand CTs as a diagnostic tool to see 'tumour' written on her pursed lips as I talked about the bending of depth perception and flickering lights.

'Can you do today?' she'd asked and I'd only been able to nod. Open on my lap was a notebook with a list of questions. The first line was just 'worse' with a question mark in bleeding purple ink.

Looking at the CT scans, I realise my rush to look at them was pointless. I wouldn't know what differentiates a healthy brain from one riddled with tumours. Against the light of the car window, my brain scans look like a butterfly mid-flight. It furls and unfurls its wings, folding them over each other.

Or perhaps, I think, it is more like a cocoon. Maybe my brain is not ill, but a caterpillar becoming a butterfly. I am swaddled in silk, safe and about to transform. My mind will flex and grow before a creature bursts forth out of me. One more beautiful and fully realised than I was ever capable of being. A creature with wings that will take me higher than I've been before. Maybe this experience is for the best, I think, because without it I could not grow. I wouldn't know the greys and whites of my own mind from which I can burst forth.

*

It's the day after seeing the psychiatrist. Hearing the news of my clear CT scan, she says if it's not epilepsy, it could be 'pseudoseizures' and I feel both relief and dread of what that means. I've already spent hours online trying to understand this diagnosis. I learn that pseudoseizures, which are now known as 'psychogenic non-epileptic seizures' or PNES, are a modern incarnation of 'hysteria'. I'm not sure what to do with this information. I'm horrified; but also, somehow, I want to laugh at these new depths of strangeness. In spite of myself, I keep reading about it. I learn that my experience is not its only incarnation, since psychosomatic symptoms, known broadly as conversion disorder, come in many forms. Seizing is just one of them, particularly physical 'grand mal' seizures, but also my own experience of focal seizures where the world shifts and changes.

Before this, I hadn't known much about hysteria. I knew that to call a woman 'hysterical' was to dismiss her. To delve into gendered assumptions of madness. But of hysteria itself, I knew only the broad strokes: that it affected women, was a label used long ago and was said to be connected to one's womb. I had thought of the word as a veil, an old label for structures of illness that are now somewhat better understood, like anxiety and schizophrenia. I had, as author Lisa Appignanesi writes in *Mad, Bad and Sad: A History of Women and the Mind Doctors from 1800 to the Present*, thought that it was an illness 'reinvented for different times' with a dramatic 'cultural malleability'. I'd never considered that I would, unwillingly, participate in the experience.

Labels are tricky things and I piece together that hysteria seems to be the absence of a diagnosis. Neurologists and psychiatrists have always doubted its existence, believing it to be a vague term that doctors can resort to when presented with a patient who is difficult to diagnose. In 1908, nosologist Armin Steyerthal said of hysteria:

> Within a few years the concept of hysteria will belong
> to history … there is no such disease and there never
> has been. What Charcot called hysteria is a tissue
> woven of a thousand threads, a cohort of the most
> varied diseases, with nothing in common but the
> so-called stigmata, which in fact may accompany any
> disease.

Yet, in 2017 when my illness takes hold, the term persists in a Google-able trail from conversion disorder. I learn that hysteria is much easier to research than conversion. I suppose this is understandable, as hysteria has been used to diagnose women – been aligned with womanhood – for centuries while the term 'conversion disorder' is significantly younger.

As psychoanalyst Neil Micklem writes in *The Nature of Hysteria*, 'Hysteria is protean: a multi-faced disease presenting such a wide variety of appearances that it has earned the reputation in some circles of being an absurd ailment with a fair proportion of incomprehensible symptoms ... [however it] projects an image consistent enough to have gained recognition as hysteria'. Micklem makes an interesting distinction: hysteria is a fluid diagnosis that throughout history has presented in varied ways. Yet, even today, when hysteria is mentioned, an image of a shaking, manic woman comes to mind.

I find a newspaper advertisement from 1932 with an image similar to the one I have in mind. A white woman is pictured with bunched-up fists pressed to her temples. Her frown is exaggerated and beneath her, in painfully large letters, reads, 'These Hysterical Women'. 'Crying ... sobbing ... laughing! She has no control of herself ... the slightest thing drives her to distraction', the ad says, espousing Lydia E Pinkham's Vegetable Compound Tablet as a cure for whatever afflicts a woman with hysteria. 'How well and happy she might be', the ad says and even though I was born over sixty years after it was printed, I want to kick something. Perhaps this is because, despite the passage of time, this perception of hysteria and madness seems to have lived on, tingeing the now. While we may no longer see words like 'she has no control of herself' as a viable way to sell a product, sick women are still told by medical professionals and bystanders alike *how well and happy they might be* if they drink water, try yoga, exercise more, sleep well, take melatonin and maybe even smile. A lot has changed; not enough has changed.

Early definitions of hysteria are very different from the way conversion disorder is seen today. The illness itself has an enduring history, one that extends back for 4000 years. In Ancient Egypt and Greece, hysteria (the Greek word for uterus is *hystera*) was thought to afflict women who had a wandering womb. The Greek physician Hippocrates was the first to use the term 'hysteria', in the fifth century BC. He believed that unlike epilepsy, which emanated from the brain, hysteria was caused by the uterus shifting in the body. Hippocrates described hysteria as especially affecting virgins, widows and single women, as he thought a sexually unsatisfied uterus could create anxiety, feelings of suffocating and convulsions, amongst other symptoms. Similarly, the Ancient Greek physician Aretaeus went on to describe the womb as 'an animal within an animal'. As such, hysteria was the illness which inspired the discipline that eventually became psychiatry.

I learn that this illness is unfathomably old. The first writing on hysteria in Egypt was the Eber Papyrus (1600 BC), the oldest medical paper on depressive disorders. The Eber Papyrus explains that to 'cure' a patient, the uterus must be returned to its original position. This was done by placing pungent substances near the woman's face and perfumed items by her vagina. This would shift the uterus downwards; if the uterus was too low in the body, the items would be switched to lift the uterus up to its rightful place.

Over time, hysteria was ascribed to various causes, from the 'wandering womb' theory to demonological reasons and finally, in the most recent history to which I belong, to psychiatric illness. The shift to religious and demonological thinking in late medieval Europe fascinates me. The era was quick to construct mental illness not as sickness but as indicating a connection between women and the Devil. The 'cure' was exorcism. Learning this, I am filled with horror at women's pain, and think with shame of my own assumptions about exorcism, built on my high school years spent watching horror movies while eating popcorn soaked in melted butter and icing sugar. Psychoanalyst Pierre Janet, speaking of the history of women with hysteria at a Harvard lecture series in 1907, said: 'Some were burnt on account of their fits or devil's claws, others were sent to prison in order to be cured of their amaurosis [loss of vision].'

I try to find a woman who lived through all this history and stumble upon one whose illness seemed to embody the political struggle between religion and science. Mary Glover. Mary was fourteen years old in London, 1602, when her illness took. Mary lived with her Puritan parents in 'litle Alhallowes in Thames streete in London', wrote physician Stephen Bradwell, the man who witnessed and then recorded her illness. Mary's home would later burn down in the Great Fire of London. Mary was a girl when she was caught between an illness and a political struggle that grew into something much greater than her own pain. Although much has been written about Mary's illness, she herself is unknown. I have no image of her to hold on to; I don't even know the colour of her hair. Her name is barely used, the words 'poor creature' often substituted. The one part in Bradwell's document that gives any hint of Mary's selfhood is when she is in the depths of her illness, experiencing much pain, and is given an orange. Bradwell writes that, 'the maide took it so kindely that she kept it in her hand, smelling ofte unto it, the most part of that day'. Through all the writing detailing every extreme and lull in her illness, I just see a young girl seeking comfort, unsure of how to live through the deep pain of her circumstances. But she also eludes me. I wonder how Bradwell copied each rushed word she prayed between her seizures. How much of this document is her and not him?

Mary first became ill after her neighbour, Elizabeth Jackson – feeling that Mary was a poor influence on her daughter – locked Mary in her home one afternoon and berated her for over an hour. Elizabeth eventually released her, but not before saying that she was 'wishing an evill death to light upon her'. From this moment, Mary experienced debilitating 'fits'. A lot is lost in transcription; the physicians who wrote about her don't care much to note the why, but focus on the symptoms they're left with.

Mary's symptoms were varied, but they were all frightening to her and her father, Tymothy, and her mother, who remains unnamed in the documents. At times, Mary's throat would close so she could not eat. She experienced intermittent low vision. During her 'fits', her body would thrash and convulse. Her side and limbs would periodically become paralysed.

Over the days, as Mary's illness worsened, her parents had the church bells ring for her in case she died. Hearing the bells, Elizabeth Jackson was heard to say to another neighbour, 'I thank my God, he hath heard my prayer, and stopped the mouth and tyed the tongue of one of myne enemies'.

Yet Mary did not die. She was kept alive, harshly, by her parents; food was forced down her throat to keep her body functioning. On two occasions, Mary fell deeply ill after seeing Elizabeth's daughter:

> She was turned rounde as a whoop [hoop], with
> her head backward to her hippes; and in that
> position rolled and tumbled, with such violence, and
> swiftness, as that their paynes in keeping her from
> receaving hurt against the bedsted, and postes, caused
> two or three women to sweat; she being all over colde
> and stiffe as a frozen thing.

Reading this, it's hard not to think of when I've been cold and stiff. Paralysed and stuck as my body temperature lowers and I can no longer feel the heat of Mathew's body beside me. And like mine, Mary's illness continued to worsen. As it did, Elizabeth was taken to the sheriff to meet with Mary. Upon seeing Elizabeth, Mary went into another 'fit'; witnesses heard a 'voice' coming from her nostrils. They interpreted the sound as a command: 'Hang her, hang her.'

The neighbourhood – as well as the church and medical community – was split. Some thought she was faking her illness, others believed Elizabeth was a witch who had cursed a young girl. 'Trials' were even staged where Elizabeth was forced to enter Mary's home and Mary would seize in response, an audience of both sceptics and Puritans crowding the room. On one occasion, the city's chief legal officer, John Croke, required a woman to enter Mary's room dressed as Elizabeth, as a test. Mary did not seize until Elizabeth, disguised in another's clothes, entered later. Croke then wished to test if Mary could experience pain, reasoning that if she was possessed, she would react. Mary was still when Croke put a hot pin to her cheek and burnt her hand with some paper he'd set alight; Croke thought she felt nothing, but I wonder if it was merely convenient for him to believe this. Movement does not indicate one's ability to feel.

The calls of 'witch' were heard and Elizabeth went to trial before the judge, Sir Edmund Anderson, at the Court of Common Pleas. Defending her as a witness was physician Edward Jorden. Jorden did not know Elizabeth or Mary personally, but hearing about Mary, he took it upon himself to testify that she was experiencing 'hysterica passio'. This illness, Jorden testified, was 'monstrous and terrible to beholde, and of such a varietie as they can hardly be comprehended within any method or boundes'. His position was firm: Mary was ill, not possessed.

Yet despite Jorden's evidence, Judge Anderson found Elizabeth guilty of witchcraft. She was sentenced: a year behind bars and she was to visit the pillory multiple times. Yet Elizabeth never served her sentence – unhappy with Anderson's judgment, various members of the community campaigned for her release. In a way, despite the trial, Elizabeth was lucky. If she had been sentenced two years later after new revisions had been added to the *Witchcraft Act*, she would have been sentenced to death.

After the trial, Jorden wrote and published a pamphlet building on his testimony. The pamphlet, *A Briefe Discourse of a Disease Called the Suffocation of the Mother*, was the first to argue that hysteria came from the brain, not the uterus. Yet his writing was ignored in favour of more traditional, Puritan views on witchcraft and possession. Although theories about hysteria had their roots in ancient medicine, few listened to or read about Jorden's thoughts.

After the trial, Mary underwent an exorcism with her parents and fellow Puritans praying by her bedside to rid her of the devil for days on end. Mary struggled through episodes of increasing pain and intensity while pastor after pastor prayed for her. In the moments when she could speak, Mary prayed for herself.

In a report written by John Swan, a divinity student, called 'A true and brief report, of the grievous vexation by Satan, or Mary Glover of Thames Street in London: and of her deliverance from the same, by the power of the Lord Jesus, blessing his own ordinance of prayer and Fasting', is this description:

There she remained without motion, her head
hanging downward, somewhat inclining towards the
shoulder, her face and colour deadly, her mouth and
eyes shut, her body stiff and senseless, so that there
were those that thought, and I think we all might
have said, 'Behold, she is dead.'

Mary remained still until in 'a moment life lifting up her
hands and stretching them wide asunder as high as she
could reach, the first word she uttered was, "He is come,
he is come"'. Her family, sitting around Mary, cried and
she began to pray, thanking God for her deliverance from
an illness she believed was evil itself.

Mary's story is hard for me to read, I think because it
is both far from and close to my own. Even more than the
difficulties and trials of her experience, it's how visceral her
pain is, vividly conveyed through the page. She begs for
not just her life, but her soul, throughout the trauma of the
exorcism and it leaves me thinking of her – almost hearing
her – as I continue to read her life. I even start to think of
the shape of her protests well after I place the books on
my shelf and close the tabs on my computer. In a way, she
follows me. Staying close in my mind, evoking both comfort and terror of what is to come.

*

You know, O Lord, my affliction, and you can help
me, for you are stronger than Satan. O Lord, now

show your strength and let us see your saving help.
Put your power to my power, and your will to my
will. Fight for me, confound his malice, destroy his
work and darken the power of Satan, and let him be
trodden under feet like dirt.

– Mary Glover's prayer during her exorcism, begging for her
'fits' to end. Witnessed by physician Stephen Bradwell.

*

Mum drives me to the beach, where my hairdresser is, the
day after the CT scan. I still smell of her, the lime scent as
rich as if I were eating the green-skinned fruit raw. I layer
it on me throughout the day. The silkiness of the oil bleeds
from my skin onto my clothes.

I sit in the hairdresser's seat for three and a half hours,
as she paints on bleach and packs it tight into foil strips
on my head. I've come here to distract myself from what's
happening in my mind but realise, too late, that I've chosen
the worst thing: to be with my own reflection for the afternoon. The wide mirror in front of me shows not only my
figure, but the illness.

The lights are strong and I can see the darkness around
my eyes. Small pinpricks for pupils. I look at the make-up I
put on that morning, bouncing a sponge thick with yellow
foundation across my cheeks. I wanted to hide the dark
circles, worn into a bruise from the two episodes I've had
within forty-eight hours. I brushed glitter across my cheek

bones in thick lines, as if iridescence could hide the illness.

I look over to the woman next to me. Her eyes are downcast and I hear her cluck and tick as she reads a copy of *Woman's Day*. My eyelids are heavy, weighted together. The droop of my head is only interrupted by a spasm of yawns. I could fall asleep right now. The episodes always suck the energy out of me, but now, the psychiatrist has put me on new drugs that make me so tired I struggle to lift a shopping bag of groceries. She said sodium valproate, an anticonvulsant and mood stabiliser, 'would help [me] whether they are seizures or pseudoseizures'.

'So, it isn't depersonalisation disorder?' I had asked her. I had read *Feeling Unreal: Depersonalization Disorder and the Loss of the Self* in a day and felt sure it described me. If I felt like an alien, what else could it be?

'No. You have a cluster of symptoms.' Her hands moved gently as she spoke, as if they were trying to soothe me. 'Depersonalisation is one of these symptoms. But DPD doesn't explain everything you've been experiencing.'

On the bus ride home, I had typed 'pseudoseizures' into a search engine. The internet wouldn't load and I sat there and looked at the blank white screen as my thumb tapped refresh over and over. My head bumped against the window as the bus swerved through the streets back to the city. I wanted to crawl into bed, but I had to spend twice as long on a bus because I wasn't driving. I would have been furious if I wasn't so deflated.

I'm brought back to myself by the bleach; packed around my ears, it begins to tingle and itch. Folds of foil stick out from the base of my skull. The hairdresser pulls out another strip. Brush, fold, scrunch. She is lost in the monotony of it and I'm grateful. I catch the woman beside me smirking at the towering foils on my head. I look like a sulphur-crested cockatoo, all pomp with towering silver feathers. When I move my head to my hand, the foil rustles as if leaves were being brushed across the street by the wind.

My thoughts flick back to what I'd learnt the day before. The psychiatrist was too busy writing notes to explain what 'pseudoseizures' meant. I think she wanted to see, for sure, if it was epilepsy before we went down that road. But if I'm seeing walls bend, how can it be 'pseudo'? Pseudo implies false. How can they be 'false' if all I want is for them to go away?

The hairdresser twists the chair so I am facing her. She lays foil across my face to do the final strips of hair across my crown. I look down into my lap as she presses silver sheets across my forehead, obstructing my vision. I try to breathe, steady long breaths like Mathew and I practise in yoga class, and that a psychologist once suggested I try when I felt a panic attack coming on. It feels as though I'm in a small cage and the scratching crinkle sound of the folding foil is amplified. I close my eyes and think of the word 'pseudo'. Could I have created the seizures? Did they begin in a small unknown part of my brain and grow into something monstrous and unstoppable?

'All done.' I open my eyes and the hairdresser looks back at me. Her eyes are circled in dark liner.

'Stay here for a moment and we'll fix you up in a second.'

I smile at her. If only it was that easy.

*

O Lord, I beseech you, look on me your poor
handmaid with the eyes of mercy. Have mercy on me
for Jesus Christ's sake. Be merciful to me and pardon
all my sins. Let them not stand up as a wall to stop
and hinder your favours from me, but wash them
all away in the death and bloodshed of Jesus Christ,
your only, true, and dear Son. I have been a vile
wretch and sinful creature, but deal not with me as I
have deserved.

– *Mary Glover, as recorded by physician Stephen Bradwell.*

*

The sodium valproate had kicked in almost immediately. I'm at a writers' group and my opinions fall out of
me, unfettered. I hate that there is no barrier between my
thoughts and my mouth. I feel sick the next day thinking
of how I spoke.

On the phone to Mum, I complain, 'I said whatever
came into my mind.' I keep thinking through every comment or idea I expressed. My own words repeat, over and
over, in my head.

'That's how it should be, love.' I hear the tone of her voice and imagine the worry embedded in her face. Her eyes crinkle just so and her lips purse slightly. She thinks she hides her worry well, but I can see it. Even when I'm not in front of her.

The drugs make me dead on my feet. I drag my soles across the pavement as I walk. My shoes scrape and I am reminded of a zombie hobbling in a deserted wasteland. I can't think clearly and I begin to nod off in public. They weren't supposed to affect me like this; the psychiatrist had said people living with bipolar had six times the amount I was taking. At the pharmacy, they presented me with two large boxes. Two hundred tablets.

'Many people are on a higher dose', the pharmacist had said, 'this is the minimum you can buy'. I added a box of dark chocolate with dried strawberries to my purchase and she'd laughed toothily.

But they were too much. Perhaps my body is more sensitive to medication than most people's. Once, after pulling the muscles in my lower back as a teenager, I'd taken Nurofen Forte. Fifteen minutes after swallowing the tablets, the sugar coating melting on my tongue as they went down, I went from lying still in pain to singing loud and clear. Mum had come into my room, worried that I had 'gone loopy'. Maybe the sodium valproate was the same; perhaps I had to build up a tolerance.

For three days, I drank five cups of coffee every day and downed mince pies that the supermarket was selling cheaply a month after Christmas. The sugar and caffeine didn't make a dent. At night, I slept a dreamless sleep for thirteen or fourteen hours. It felt as though I was in the land of the dead.

The next day, after an afternoon lie-down and four cups of coffee, I found enough energy to call a neurologist to book in a brain scan. The psychiatrist had said I needed an EEG, a test which detects epileptic seizures. To move forward in any treatment plan, I had to know whether I needed anticonvulsants, or to somehow address the question mark next to 'pseudoseizures'. I am caught between two paths and without an EEG, I cannot navigate which way will lead me to health.

I lay my notebook on the bed with the neurologist's number scrawled on one page, a pen resting in the crook of its fold. Before dialling, I take a moment to steady myself. I need to sound alert, not as if I have been sleeping for the past week. The office assistant answers on the third ring and I will my voice to be taut, in contrast to my body, slumped against the wall.

'Hi … hello, when is your next available appointment for an EEG?'

'Do you mean an E-C-G or E-E-G?' She speaks slowly, stretching out the words as if I cannot understand them, but her tone is impatient.

'EEG – to measure the electrical activity in my brain. My GP wanted me to ring up and enquire where there is the smallest wait time before she writes a referral. Although I already have a referral for the RAH.'

Her reply is quick. 'I cannot say without your referral.'

I'm slow to reply, taking a breath and trying to clear the fog of meds. 'I don't need to book an appointment now, I was just wondering roughly what the wait time is. Like, a week or two or months?' I leave the question hanging.

She says it again, 'I cannot say without a referral'.

'I could send you the referral to the hospital if that helps? It says "EEG".'

'No. It needs to be to us.'

The tiredness is setting in, so I tell her goodbye. As I place the phone down on my mattress, I burst into tears, the kind that splatter onto the floorboards and turn your pillow cool and damp.

I cry for a minute or so. It exhausts me and once again I fall asleep. I sleep through the late afternoon, through the evening, and so dinner passes me by. I wake up late, Mathew now sleeping beside me in the bed. I get out of bed; the house is dark and the fuzz of my mind makes it hard to navigate without bumping into doorways. I go to the kitchen to take the valproate. I've slept through my reminder alarm. I flick on the light and my eyes burn. I reach for the box, a bulky thing with rows and rows of blister packs. On it, there is a diagram: an outline of a person's head with a wave surging through their brain in red.

The pills themselves are a pastel purple. I remember reading about the psychology of how pharmaceutical companies colour medication. Red is supposed to bring to mind thoughts of quick, fast-acting medication (think Nurofen) while blue is to calm us. Perhaps purple would be a mix of the two; fast-acting mood stabilisers. I'm not sure, but the pastel unnerves me. It is more the colour of a child's bedspread than a mind-altering medication.

I try to take it. The pill brushes my lips but I can't bear to put it in my mouth. It feels like a death sentence for another day. A day of feeling as though there is no life force in me, that I am here to sleep. I later learn I am in the 4 per cent of people on this medication who experience fatigue and the 1 per cent who feel pain (mine manifested in thumping headaches that grew worse when I moved). For me, taking this medication makes me feel not myself, or anyone else. It is to live as a shell.

I stop taking them – I feel as if I have no choice – and the fatigue fades. As I come back into myself, I realise I've had a glimpse into another world of mental illness. A world where antidepressants and therapy are not the answer but psych wards and constantly changing meds are routine. I realise I've shifted in to a deeper world of mental health-care. One that perhaps I already inhabited but wasn't prepared to confront.

Over the coming days, the effects of the stabilisers fade. I announce loudly and with a fat grin to Mathew one morning, 'I'm back. It's me.' He is sitting down, lacing up his sneakers methodically before a run. He looks up, shocked and realising I'm right. That day, I don't yawn but I still sleep in thick doses at night. The next day, I feel as though I am fully myself.

I realise, as I come back into myself, that being told to take your meds is a theme in the lives of the mentally ill. To stop is to be 'stupid', to risk yourself. But that positions doctors as all-knowing; their prescription pad knows best. That's not always true. Doctors try out meds to see what works: it is a lucky dip into a drawer of prescription medications. They don't always believe patients who complain about how bad the side-effects are – they can't comprehend that sometimes the meds are worse than the illness they are there to help. Stopping meds can be a bad decision, but it can also be the best. In my experience, it is not as simple as the medical world paints it to be.

It's also true that not all meds are created equal, at least when it comes to my own experience of side-effects. The antidepressants I've been on for five years have helped – and the side-effects of heightened concentration and nausea were bearable until they faded after a couple of weeks. But there is only so much I can take: literally. I have reached the maximum dose my psychiatrist will allow due to the wild card of my heart murmur. And the pills only help so much; I find myself yo-yoing between hating the hole in my heart and realising the point is moot. While they take the edge off my illness, I'm barely surviving, even with them boosting my serotonin levels.

Once the valproate moves out of my system, I feel the creep of anxiety come back. It's as though, without the mask of sedatives, the anxiety looms on the periphery. Always there, watching me and waiting to rush in. I feel unsteady within myself. Scared, even, that at any moment a seizure could come. That a seizure could wash over me and, once again, I will lose myself.

*

Unlike with Edith, as I read about Mary I find I'm stuck on the differences between us rather than the similarities. Mary was saved. She was revived from a life of illness that paralysed her limbs and made her throat gurgle. She eventually turned away from physicians and believed in prayer, in God and perhaps most of all, in being forgiven. I am not a believer and so I cannot be saved. I do not believe in either God or the devil. For me, a concept of 'evil' doesn't explain anything, and 'good' promises no cure.

In one way, I feel a deep pity for Mary. She writhed and twisted in pain for days as she was surrounded by prayer. She believed she and her family were rotten, that she was being rightly punished. But Mary was healed. She overcame her possession; she was delivered into a life without illness. And for that, I envy her deeply.

*

I talk to Dad about conversion disorder. I trust him. Not just because he is my parent but because of his keen insight into the world. He is one of the smartest, most measured people I know. In another life, he would have been a psychiatrist instead of a barrister. In his free hours, he teaches himself Arabic, French, Italian and Greek. Dad now composes music, spurred on by his cousin Andrew. When Andrew was admitted into a nursing home, Dad would transcribe his handwritten music to a computer program so that he could hear it back in the last years of his life. The habit stuck and he continues to write music, for himself.

Dad looks like the kind of man you'd expect to hold old-fashioned opinions. He wears suits and embroidered polo shirts, has a mess of thick white hair and towers at over six feet tall. People tend to assume he holds the conservative values often aligned with his generation, that he is proper and uptight. But he dislikes people who are fastidious about grammar or speak down to others. He drives a wreck; the side mirror is held together by tape. He refuses a new car, while his colleagues drive glossy grey things, as it works just fine.

He is not only smart but kind, so I ask him why this is happening to me. It feels odd to ask; it's a return to childhood. When he used to drive me to school, he would ask me for advice: 'Why do people get angry and yell so quickly?' I remember feeling so proud because when I spoke he truly listened to what I had to say. He would lean over as he drove, his shoulder tilted down so he could be close to each of my words. I felt that my opinions were valued and important.

Now, I feel like a kid again. But one without an opinion. Just like when I was little, he's driving. As we drive away from my appointment, the corners make me nauseous. The air conditioner is on high even though the sun is barely out. I ask him what he thinks of my illness. He takes a moment before speaking.

'Did I ever tell you about a friend of mine and his cough?'

My mind is blank. 'No?'

'Well, this man has always been seen as the baby of the family. And, incorrectly, he is seen as the least successful. It was always academia for those around him but he could go to a college of some type.'

I'm nodding as he speaks. 'I hate these false mythologies families perpetuate about each other. They can be so damaging.' I turn the air conditioner down two switches.

'Yes, and so, when he is surrounded by old school chums, it brings back these things. On two occasions, I remember two guys were talking about something vaguely intellectual. They didn't speak down to him, but didn't include him in any way. He started having an awful coughing fit. Had to leave. And I've spoken with him about this before, and he admits he has never had these fits otherwise.' He looks over to me, holding eye contact for a moment before his eyes flick back to the road ahead. 'You can Google it. It's known as psychological coughing.'

'O-kay. But why a cough?'

'Well, although unconscious, it provides a tangible benefit. Someone can excuse themselves from the room and does not have to participate in the conversation.' Dad shifts gears and the car jerks a little.

'That makes sense. But what about me? How does it benefit me to have seizures? Especially in front of other people. I don't have a tangible benefit, I just feel frightened.' My words come out quickly and I am left breathless.

Dad twists the steering wheel in a smooth movement to accommodate the bend of the road.

'Well', he pauses. I imagine he's thinking his words through so they come out just right. 'You, I think, are the kind of person who sees a lot in the world. But maybe you see too much, like Virginia Woolf did. It becomes painful.' He nods at his words. 'This could be your brain taking you out of the world, for a little while.'

I think of *Orlando* where Woolf writes: 'All extremes of feeling are allied with madness.' Maybe this extreme, the seizures, are not entirely madness but a protection of sorts.

'Hmm. Maybe you're right. When it happens, I feel removed from the world. I don't have a self and cannot recognise my own street or even my hands.'

Dad nods, now quiet. I look at the soft wrinkles under his eyes and think of the tears that might be blooming in mine.

'I don't know whether I want this to be epilepsy or conversion. Epilepsy, although the medication is confronting, is clear cut. But with conversion, I don't know where to begin.'

I look at Dad; my hands are twisting over themselves in my lap. If it was normal for us, I'd lean into his shoulder for comfort. But we don't hug and I busy myself with wringing my hands. His eyes stay on the road.

When he speaks, his voice comes out gentle. 'Let's hope for conversion. We can work through it. Resolve it. Epilepsy presents some complications that you don't want.'

I know he means the drugs I'll have to take if it's epilepsy, the side-effects. But it scares me to think I might be mad. It feels easier to go through the hard option because then, I think, I'll stay intact. I nod after his words, so slowly he might not catch it.

'Okay, Dad.'

And for a moment, I push out the feelings of madness. Taking the next bend with Dad, with the crackle of the car's engine, the future begins to feel a little clearer.

*

And hereupon the *Symptoms* of this disease are fayd to be monstrous and terrible to beholde, and of such a varietie as they can hardly be comprehended within any method or boundes. Insomuch as they which are ignorant of the strange affects which naturall causes may produce, and of the manifold examples which our profession of Phificke doth minister in this kind, have fought aboue the Moone for supernaturall causes: ascribing there accidents either to diabolicall possession, to witchcraft, or to the immediate finder of the Almightie.

– A Brief Discourse of a Disease *by Edward Jorden*.

*

What confounds me about my episodes is how quickly I can come out of them, back into everyday life. Back to happiness. Dancing with Mathew, Suzie following our spindly arms and shaking butts around the house, as we

listen to the Pixies or the jazz that all sounds like one long
song to me. Laughing with Mum and Dad about a game of
Cluedo where we send Mathew, who is much too good at
the game, back to his start space for the second time.

The ability to slip back into my own life, at first, makes
me think it's epilepsy. But then, the puzzle pieces start to fit
together. The first episodes came loose and quick. I wrote
of that first month:

> As I dragged soaped sponges against plates, watched
> grains of rice fatten in starchy water and collected
> an inbox of rejection slips, my body began to crack.
> At first it was so small to be imperceptible, cracks
> running up me like the crease of a dog-eared page.
>
> By the time I noticed they were deep, they snaked
> their way down through layers of skin. I began to
> walk clutching my middle, scared of what could
> fall out. I fidgeted through sleep. The world began
> to fuzz at the edges, like the fraying of an old bed
> sheet. I felt less and less a part of life outside my
> front door.

Although I write lightly of rejection slips, I'm not being
forthright. I remember feeling unhappy, but it's so easy to
blur it in my memory. Funny though that I could forget
what it's like, when at the time, it felt like the blood was
pouring out of me. It's supposed to be impossible to fully
remember the experience of pain – it is meant to account

for why women can bear childbirth again and again – and, I think, this is true of mental illness, too.

I remember: August was a month of waiting. After talking to a publisher about working together on a book and not hearing back for seven months, I crack. The stress of compulsively checking emails, starting to believe I am not and will never be 'good', undoes me. The idea had haunted me through high school and here it was, once again, following me.

I think back on this time with a vague sense of anxiety. I thought there were some good times, some bad – but Mathew corrects me. He says I would come to him, nerves alive and tense, and say what a worthless person I was. He is shocked I don't remember. I was not in a good place, to put it lightly.

But regardless of the intensity of the stress I felt tensing and pulsating through my stomach muscles, how could this be enough to awaken non-epileptic seizures? It seems ridiculous. CS Lewis said, 'Failures are finger posts on the road to achievement.' And stand-up comedian Carol Leifer said, 'As a writer, the worst thing you can do is work in an environment of fear of rejection.' I agree with them. Often, rejection doesn't really affect me. I've been on both ends of publishing – writing and editing – and I know there are many reasons why a piece is rejected, not solely that the writing is bad. So why the seizures? Was it because this was my first book? Or that writing had grown into a part of the way I saw myself, a part of my very consciousness? If I could not be a writer, what was my purpose?

In writing circles, you are encouraged not to conflate writing and the self. You are *not* your writing. In chronic illness communities, you are encouraged similarly. You are *not* your illness. But on any given day, I feel like a strand of yarn woven with the things that make me a person. My writing is a part of me. My illness (whether epilepsy or conversion), too, has become a part of me. It is not the only part; I am also a partner, a daughter, a knitter, a good cook, a coffee drinker, an average chess player and someone who buys too many books. But the illness and the writing run deep. I have had OCD since I was seven; I began writing when I was seventeen; I had my first panic attack on my eighteenth birthday. I cannot push these ideas away as if they are separate to my self.

Siri Hustvedt discusses the self and illness as intertwined in her memoir of her convulsions, *The Shaking Woman*. She writes:

> Every sickness has an alien quality, a feeling of
> invasion and loss of control that is evident in the
> language we use about it. No one says, 'I am cancer'
> or even 'I am cancerous,' despite the fact there is no
> intruding virus or bacteria; it's the body's own cells
> that have run amok. One *has* cancer. Neurological
> or psychiatric illnesses are different, however,
> because they often attack the very source of what
> one imagines is one's self. 'He's an epileptic' doesn't
> sound strange to us. In the psychiatric clinic, the
> patients often say, 'Well, you see, I'm bipolar' or

'I'm schizophrenic.' The illness and the self are fully identified in these sentences.

I know I'm neurotic. I'm anxious, too. But now, after six months of seizures, can I call myself a person living with epilepsy? Or a PNES-sufferer? I wonder whether the seizures will help me step back, draw breath. I like to think my body tells me what it needs.

But again and again, I contemplate if I can bear to add another diagnosis to a growing list. I'd like to think my body is speaking to me but I'm not sure I can listen to it. Not if it's telling me I'm ill, again and with increasing severity. I'm beginning to feel more like a collector than a person. I carry the diagnoses with me as I move through the world, and like iron weights strapped onto me, they pull me down.

*

O Lord, though you would let Satan kill my body, let him have no power over my soul.

– *Mary Glover, witnessed by Stephen Bradwell.*

*

It doesn't take long before my family and I start joking about the seizures. How quickly they went from something we didn't talk about – something wild and feared

– to this. I guess sadness and empathy are not all there is to living and feeling chronic illness. It becomes everyday. A part of me, and a joke.

When Yiayia was dying from bowel cancer, living through cycles of chemo and radiation, she would shake. It made it hard for her to do things she used to love like knitting, and one Christmas when I was fifteen, she asked me to wrap her presents. I sat on the spotless beige carpet in her lounge room as we watched the news together. My wrapping was fastidious. I needed edges and sealed corners. I remember the sounds of pulling cellotape taut punctuating our conversation over the news.

On Christmas Day, Yiayia asked my little cousin to hand out her presents. They were so tightly wrapped, everyone struggled to open them. It took three times as long as usual. We all laughed hard, harder than the occasion deserved. I remember looking at Yiayia's big grin and how her thick gold hoop earrings swayed from side to side as she laughed. Increasingly, little things began to stand out as her body shrank from the treatment.

I can't remember if that was her last Christmas. It might have been, or perhaps it was the last one she was well enough to be fully herself. Christmas was always her time of year. She loved the colourful lights and corny decorations, dancing Santas and all. That moment is one of my favourite memories of her, and us. The joy of it was not tainted by her terminal illness. While painful for all of us, her sickness had become a part of her.

The same is beginning to happen with me. One night

Mathew and I are playing Cluedo with Mum and Dad. Our dogs, both leggy greyhounds, sleep next to each other on two armchairs. Suzie is curled tight and symmetrical as a ring on the brown armchair. Ginnie spreads herself long, taking up most of the three-seater. Stuffing peeks out from under her chin; she's seventeen months old but still likes to chew. She's already chewed five of Dad's belts in half.

The table of the Cluedo sheet – the lines stacked up – begin to blur. I blink to straighten their appearance but the room spins a little. By my side, I see Mum with her phone. She is taking a photo of the dogs sleeping peacefully together. I can't quite see the shape of her. I hear Mathew, his voice liquid, and I can't quite fixate on it.

'What did you say?'

'Colonel Mustard with the axe in the spa.'

I look back down to my sheet. The lines are less blurred. I begin to answer Mathew's question but Dad interrupts.

'Hey, didn't you already have a turn?'

Mum joins in. 'Yeah', she exclaims. 'You said Plum, bat, spa.'

Mathew starts to laugh; his body flexes back in his chair.

'Well, I had to try. You were taking photos. Tim was caught up in his score sheet. And Katie was having one of her episodes.' His hand waves loosely in my direction.

Mum and I start to lose it. The laughter comes heavy and quick. I buckle over, my face scrunched against the Cluedo sheet as I bang my hand against the table. We laugh so hard, we forget whose turn it is.

This is what illness becomes. It grows from this small

thing inside of you until it morphs and fills you up, stretching into every crevice. It's frightening at first but then the fear dulls and you are left with it; the illness and you, the boundaries of one from the other blurred.

Cory Taylor writes in *Dying: A memoir* about her experience of realising her own consciousness as a child:

> I saw a kookaburra swoop down from a branch to
> spear a skink and gobble it down live. This is what
> dragged me out of unconsciousness. This is me here,
> I thought, and that is you there, and where there was
> a skink there is nothing.

Laughing at the Cluedo board was a coming into consciousness. Not of my own existence as separate to the things around me, nor the realisation of my own death, but a consciousness of my illness. Laughing as I did, I realised that to be ill was normal. The seizures morphed from a disturbance to a fixed state of being. A state that I now navigate my life with.

*

> Come to me all you that are weary and laden, and I
> will ease you.
>
> – *Matthew 11.28, read to Mary by 'the second preacher' as
> documented by John Swan.*

*

On a 41°C day, my phone rings. It's the Royal Adelaide Hospital. They've had a cancellation and can I come in today? It's a month before my appointment and the thought of an EEG has been ticking over in my head constantly. I tell them I'll be there at two. They ask that I wash my hair beforehand, no conditioner. Just shampoo.

I arrive ten minutes early. Mum is with me. I'm still not driving; my vision still isn't steady enough for me to feel I can get behind the wheel safely. Mum is carrying a clear blue folder of articles to read on materiality in social and cultural geography while she waits for my EEG to be over. My face is a question mark when she tells me this.

'What's materiality?'

She pauses for a long moment, trying to think of a way to simplify it for me. As her face squirms, I start to smile.

'Never mind,' I tell her.

Mum opens the folder and I can hear the out-breath of Velcro being pulled apart. I look around the hospital from the clean couch we've been seated on. The neurology unit is on the top floor and I had to block my peripheral vision as we walked over to the unit; I couldn't bear to look at all of the glass-walled wards beneath us. From where I sit, I can see a small patch of bright sky. The wall across from us is wallpapered with a long photo of a beach. The shoreline leads up to a white frothy ocean. The grass on the dunes looks slightly pixelated from where I sit.

The Royal Adelaide opened a few months ago. The

building is connected to the medical research centre, a quadrilateral of knotted metal, and looks like a spaceship. It has been met with a lot of public animosity. But I quite like the oddness of it on Adelaide's small city skyline. New buildings as interesting and alien as this are few in South Australia.

Inside, it's much like the array of hospitals I've visited throughout my life: a place of muted tones and linoleum floors. The only difference is that it hasn't yet had a chance to accumulate a blanket of scuff marks from gurneys and the thick-heeled shoes of healthcare workers.

Looking at the walls, I notice the man sitting next to us. His hair is white and he is resting his bare feet on top of a pair of black rubber thongs. He jiggles his toes back and forth. I watch them sway for a moment, feeling as though my body is swaying with them, before I overhear the receptionist on the phone.

'Yes, can you ask her to wash her hair beforehand? Just shampoo. Nothing else. Make sure it's dry.'

My hand instinctively goes to feel the roots of my hair. Is it cool because of the strong flow of air conditioning within the hospital walls or is it still damp from the wash?

'Mum, feel my head.'

She turns. I wonder if she, too, has been listening to the receptionist or if she's lost in the world of materiality. Her face looks as though she's thinking, jokingly, 'Get lost' at my request (this is something she likes to say more often than you would imagine an academic well into tenure would). She feels my head.

She nods, confirming. 'It's damp.'

'Shit', I whisper in a low voice, 'do you think it'll be a problem?'

A woman comes around the bend of the hospital corridor. Her hair is short and neat and she's dressed in a yellow and green floral dress that, for a reason that's beyond me, brings the word 'verbena' to mind. Behind her, an elderly woman walks with a slightly strange gait. Her walker blends into the light grey colour of the hospital walls. My vision blurs a little as I gaze at the peach of her shoes.

Verbena walks up to me. 'You must be Katerina.'

I think I nod or smile, not managing to speak. I can feel the nerves running up my shoulders and arms. Verbena smiles and I look at the smudge of black eyeliner around the green of her eyes. She introduces herself, but my nerves are humming now and I forget her name immediately. I remind myself not to call her Verbena out loud.

'Follow me,' she says.

She walks quickly and I struggle to keep her pace in my Birkenstocks. She shows me into a room overlooking distant parklands. I look at the stretching angles of the gum trees and wonder where else I would be if it weren't for the episodes. What does one do on a summer's day?

I sit in a chair Verbena points to and she begins grooming me for the procedure. First, she combs through my hair with a tortoiseshell plastic comb, and I can hear the scrape and vibration of it brushing against my scalp. Verbena stretches her arm in front of me, showing a blue-latexed hand. She runs a red pencil over the back of her hand, drawing a small cross.

'I'm going to make these marks across your head, so you'll feel a sensation.'

I try not to laugh at the thought of red medical crosses being marked onto my scalp; the symbols don't belong on a head that defies the medical industry's definitions of illness. I ask Verbena about the type of pencil to distract myself from my mess of thoughts. She tells me it's an ordinary pencil and we settle into the silence as she marks my head. The pencil feels exactly as you would imagine: a rough scratch against your skull that brings back memories of school and piles of eraser residue. Verbena then takes a wet ear bud and rubs the pencil marks vigorously, all nineteen of them. I imagine the effect is blurred red dots, like chicken pox, running up my skull.

'So, tell me your story', she says. 'What brings you here?'

I relay my illness, tired of it by now: the stretching walls and distorted faces of my seizures. I can't see her face – she is standing directly behind me – but I can feel the soggy push of the cotton spreading from my right ear to the left. Her vigorous rubbing does not pause as I talk.

When I've finished, mentioning the specific peculiarities of my vision, I end with a sigh and a deflated 'Yeah'. Verbena is silent for a moment. The drawing and rubbing, drawing and rubbing continues.

'Huh', she says in a rising tone as if it were a question.

I don't know how to take this, so I probe her. 'Different, right?'

'Well ...' The pencil hits the peak of my skull. 'We're all individuals with different brains. Seizures present themselves differently in everyone.'

I take that to be a yes. It *is* different. There is a pause in the conversation and Verbena walks over to the other side of the room, pulling a trolley with a little black machine and long swooping cords. This is the first time I've seen her in twenty minutes and I watch her sterilising the cords with an antiseptic wipe while my head keeps tingling from the rubbing. My scalp feels as though a hairdresser has been too rough scrubbing the dye out of my hair.

Verbena then takes out an electrode, placing it against her finger so I can see it clearly.

'See that metal part?'

It's copper and the shape of a shrunken, flat traffic cone. I nod.

'I'm going to glue that onto you and then tape it down with this.' She shows me a strand of wispy cotton medical tape. 'Then, I might also use your hair to make sure the electrodes are fully stuck.'

The glue is cold against my skull and the task is laborious. She tells me she knows the glue is awkward; just yesterday, a colleague had practised a technique on her. Her hair had become greasy and slick from the procedure.

'So,' I begin, my mouth dry and nervous to hear her answer, 'when will I see the results?'

'Well, a neurologist will review the brain wave recording, either in real time or after the procedure. They will write a report and send it through to your GP. So, it will take ten to fourteen days. Depending on how busy they are.'

I exhale, quick and exasperated. I don't mean to show my frustration, but I know those fourteen days will undo me. Wondering about whether I have epilepsy or a diagnosis which is much more slippery.

'That's longer than I expected,' I say.

Verbena tells me she understands. She says I'm at a crossroads. Her hands stop weaving through my hair and pressing the metal cone deep into my skin. She walks around my chair to face me.

'You're waiting to hear which path to go down.' Her palms join together in a 'V' shape.

I smile. 'Yes.'

After the electrodes are secure, she asks me to stand and walk to a plush green leather recliner chair in the centre of the room. It's hard to believe that the test has not yet begun; I look at my watch. Forty minutes have passed. As I walk, the electrodes and their colourful wires fall around me like a mane of hair. I walk slowly, so as not to disturb them, and my measured, dipping steps remind me of a bride walking down the aisle with an electrode veil.

Once I'm in the chair, Verbena presses a lever and I'm taken back. My feet are swooped up in the recliner's arch and my head sinks further into the chair's deep cushion.

'Okay, now I'm going to close the blinds and dim the lights.'

The room gradually grows darker and I flick my feet back and forth absentmindedly. A Birkenstock almost flies off my foot and I grow still, except for running my thumb over the ridges of my nails to release nervous energy.

Verbena walks over to the computer and makes a few assured clicks.

'Okay, we're going to begin. This should take twenty minutes. Close your eyes please. Let your shoulders sink down and let your jaw relax.'

I do as she says, realising as she speaks how hard I've been gripping my jaw. The molars were fixed and pressing together tightly.

With my eyes closed, I can still hear the occasional click of Verbena's hand and I imagine the movement of my brain waves growing and shrinking. She had said earlier that they would make eighteen drops and spikes each second.

'Eyes open.' Her tone has changed. She has switched from polite questions to commands. I notice that her voice is loud and each syllable is overly pronounced, as if she thinks I might have fallen asleep or am no longer able to understand her.

I look at the room, my eyes adjusting to the low light. Across from me is an orange office chair. It reminds me of the chairs at primary school, where teachers would sit to address us, sitting quiet and cross-legged on the floor. From the seat falls a long orange thread. It dangles, unmoving. I stare at it from where I'm glued, unable to move and wanting to pull each electrode from my scalp. I fantasise about walking over to the chair and with a swift rip, removing the wispy thread.

The tingle of the glue has turned into an itch. The

electrodes behind my ears become unbearable. I grip my hands, fingers interlocking, so tight that it hurts. I think of being eleven and lice spreading to me from a school friend, again and again. She did nothing while every weekend I spent an hour by the sink as Mum pulled and tugged at the knots in my hair. By Tuesday, the lice would be back and my scalp would return to itching. At the beginning of each school day, I'd brush my long hair and look down at the brown cable-knit school jumper. The jumper would swirl and twitch, lice hurrying back up to my head.

'Eyes shut.' A pause. 'Can you open your mouth, as wide as possible?'

I stretch my mouth out. The action pulls at my lips, which are dry from the summer's day. I think of Edvard Munch's *The Scream*. Didn't I read somewhere that the painting is thought to show the experience of depersonalisation?

'You're doing great.' But Verbena's tone doesn't encourage me. It still feels commanding. I wonder how long it has been.

My jaw is starting to ache, tongue twisting within the confines of my mouth. What do you do with your tongue when your mouth is spread open like this? It feels unnatural and the more I try to press it down, the more it springs up at odd, tight angles. This sense of unfamiliarity with my own body always happens at the dentist too. I begin to question the natural way of things.

'Close mouth. Eyes open.'

Verbena's voice is loud and clear. It's as if she went to a

training seminar on how to instruct patients effectively but with the least human touch possible: Eyes. Open. Eyes. Shut. I think of what it would be to live like this, Verbena following me around and telling me how to live. 'Breathe in, breathe out. Boil the kettle. Feed the dog.' A small smile appears on my lips and once again, I notice the wriggling presence of my own tongue.

'Eyes closed. Now, slowly, move your neck up so it is no longer on the chair. You're going to breathe in and out using only your mouth. Don't breathe from your nose. This will happen for three minutes. It's called hyperventilating. Some people feel a bit breathless and dizzy. That's normal. In fact, that means you're doing a good job.'

I'm not ready to hear this. I had spent the hour or two between the phone call and arriving at the hospital reading about EEGs. I'd been prepared for small tests. Maybe, my hopeful mind thought, they'll ask me to complete a puzzle. Saying this to Mum after the EEG, she had looked at me quizzically before saying, 'They're not testing your brain function.' I snap back at her, 'Well I know that now.'

I start breathing in and out. Verbena follows along with me for the first three breaths. I'm afraid that this will trigger a panic attack, not that I've hyperventilated since my GP put me on antidepressants years ago. Sometimes, though, I feel myself getting close to those shallow, out-of-control breaths. There's one hill at my old university that would always set me off. The steepness would make my head rush, my sneakers struggling to grip the worn-down bitumen. I would puff and pant up it, pausing and pretending to look at a text on my phone to catch my breath and calm myself out of an attack.

'Halfway. You're doing a great job.'

The breathing has started to affect me now. Wooziness spreads through my head. I feel light and my brain tingles. It reminds me of the giddy feeling Mathew and I got when we first met and he decided to buy a coffee plunger to replace his oversized tin of Nescafé Blend 43. We had misread the instructions and piled eight overflowing spoons of ground beans into the shining glass receptacle. We drank it all and our hands shook, together, as we gripped each other's fingers. The feel of his hands, the soft skin without calluses, was still unfamiliar to me then.

'Okay. Great work. Sit back and rest.'

I hear the squeak of a machine being wheeled towards me. I want to open my eyes, glance at what Verbena's doing, but will a peek interfere with the test? I can't do this again, I think and so I scrunch my eyes closed, gritting my teeth as I resist the urge to look. As I sit through the test, I notice the heaviness in my limbs. The softness of the chair triggers a familiar relaxation in my muscles. Maybe it was the hyperventilation, but I begin to feel tired. I start to rub my thumb over the knuckles of my left hand, feeling each groove carefully, concentrating on staying fully conscious.

I can sense Verbena lowering the machine, adjusting it carefully, so it sits right in front of my face. I cannot see it, but I still feel smothered and sick at its presence.

'I'm going to turn on some lights now. Eyes shut.'

The light flashes slowly at first, like the measured blink of a walk signal at a traffic light. Then it begins to quicken. It flashes for a few seconds at each pace until it flashes so quickly it appears to be a sustained bright light. From behind my eyelids, I see rich pinks morphing to orange as the brightness grows. It's a shock and while the clicking of the flash speeds up, I forget to breathe.

The flash stops and suddenly, the room feels cool again. I take a breath.

'Eyes open.'

Looking at the room, it's a grey blur. My eyes take a long moment to adjust. I look to the small window on the door, blinds clasped shut. There are boxes of blue surgical gloves stacked upon one another. Next to them, a large purple can of air freshener. Lavender. I imagine its scent.

'Now, I'm going to turn the light on again. Don't look at the light, look past it towards the wall.'

I fixate on the orange chair. With my blurred vision, I can no longer see the orange thread. Instead, I look at the thick foam padded seat. Between the seat and the back, there is a curving piece of black plastic. It's ribbed and looks like a plastic spine.

Verbena turns on the lights again. They come quickly, with increasing strength. The brightness is overwhelming and I can feel my face contorting. My eyes become slits; my mouth stretching out in pain. I feel the soft touch of water running from my eyelids down my cheeks.

The lights stop.

'Eyes shut. Don't move your face.' Her voice is tense

now. 'The muscles in your face are strong. They can override the signal from your brain waves.'

Strips of light rush and blur behind my eyelids. I murmur in response. I think of Dad in hospital last year. After coming out of the anaesthetic, he'd become paranoid. In the Intensive Care Ward, volunteers sit with patients as they come into consciousness. An elderly woman had sat, knitting and waiting for him to come to. 'I hated that woman,' he said to me. I laughed, a hard bark. Dad sounded serious and I'd never heard his voice laced with such poison. The anaesthesia had made him paranoid. He knows this, but his hate of the knitting woman continues to this day. I feel similarly about Verbena in this moment. The light is so painful in my eyes the room is spinning. How can she tell me not to wrinkle my face?

The flickering starts again. As it grows in intensity, the shimmering orange heat waves behind my eyes grow and spread. They morph into a towering ball of orange wool, fuzzy around the edges. As quickly as it came, the light stops. Darkness.

'Eyes open.'

I've begun to hate opening my eyes; it's far more bearable with a thin slip of skin between me and the lights. As the lights flicker, growing faster and faster, what I can see grows smaller. The span of the room – the big wall, the blue latex gloves, the orange chair – narrows until I am left with a pinprick of black, surrounded by white nothing. My heart quickens in panic.

I remember the dream I once had where I could not

see. I had tried to walk home, barefoot and alone, only to fall in a pile of thick brambles. I remember wondering, as I slept, whether I had the resilience to stand up and move forward.

The light stops. 'Eyes shut.' A pause as my eyes adapt to the darkness. I hear Verbena clicking.

'You've done such a good job. All done now.' Her tone is still firm but some of that softness from our earlier conversation seeps through.

As she walks around the room, opening blinds and flicking switches, she starts to talk. I'm not sure what she is saying; I am dazed from the lights. I look at myself in the soft reflection in the glass window of the door. I cannot see myself clearly but the outline is of someone foreign all the same. Snaking cords run down my shoulders. I am not myself; I feel imaginary, a being from science fiction.

The dizziness becomes worse and I lean my head over into my lap, clasping my face with my hands. My fingertips graze the cones glued to the edges of my forehead. They are covered in soft tape, hard underneath. I've felt mad before, but this is the first time I feel sick.

I walk over to the chair at Verbena's instruction, careful to be steady and slow on my feet. She plucks off the electrodes, one by one. She scrubs at the patches of glue on my head as though I were a stove top, not a person. Taking off the electrodes is much quicker than attaching them, but more uncomfortable.

I am allowed to leave. I follow Verbena out of the room into the hospital hallway, not trying to keep up with her stride. I walk slowly, watching the nurses rush around me. Visitors look from room to room, trying to find their families. I realise we have been in the room for well over an hour.

Verbena takes me to Mum. I see her before she sees me. Her glasses are lifted up onto the crown of her head and she is holding her phone close, two inches or so from her face. She is frowning and I know immediately what she is doing. She is worried and as we both do when anxious, obsessively Googling how long I might be in that room with the bright lights. She looks up and sees me. I try my best not to look sick and dizzy and Mum smiles.

It's over. Now, I must wait. Mum leads me back through the hallway, down the elevator, to the car. I follow her weakly, letting her take me to the comfort of home.

*

The Land is full of Witches, they abound in all places … Divines [and] Phisitions, I know they are learned and wise, but to say this is naturall, and tell me neither the cause, nor the Cure of it, I care not for your Judgement.

— *Sir Edmund Anderson, judge at Elizabeth Jackson's trial.*

*

I'm finding myself becoming uncomfortably angry. The seizures are *real*. Whether it's conversion or epilepsy – and I still don't know where I sit – the two present in the same way. The dichotomy is slippery between them but when I explain what's happening in my brain to those closest to me, we revert to talking about the seizures being 'real' or 'fake'.

One day is particularly tough. Mathew is sick, nausea flooding in the night before. He wakes well – thankfully – but tired and with a thick pile of readings to do for his degree. The night before, he asked me to cover his tutoring shift. I agreed, my hand resting on his stomach as he groaned in a dark room. The next day I wake to the sound of him playing the piano. 'Clair de Lune', maybe. I wrench myself out of bed; the previous day I'd worked a nine-hour shift and I was still feeling the ache in my feet and lower back.

We have breakfast together: me, coffee and him, yoghurt. We talk about how he's feeling (better but anxious about the work he missed) and what I need to run through with his year nines (narrative writing and structure). We sit in the quiet for a moment. I swallow the last of my coffee, wrinkling my nose at the cold dregs.

'So, when shall we leave?'

'We?' he frowns.

'I thought you were driving?'

'Driving you to work? Why?'

'Because I can't drive. The seizures.'

'You're not driving?'

My anger swells. 'I haven't been driving for weeks!'

'Well, if I'd known I had to drive you, why would I ask you to cover my shift?' He's exasperated now.

'I don't know. I thought you wanted more time to study.' I don't want to fight. When we do, I hate the liminal space I live in afterwards. Not sure if I can reach out and touch his arm, whether the fight has yet ended.

I continue, softer. 'It's not safe if I drive right now.'

'But I thought it was conversion,' he says, his voice softer too.

'I don't know for sure yet. And even if it is, they're still real seizures.' I keep my voice quiet. I try not to yell the words at him. But despite the softness in my voice, the words keep circling in my head with a sense of growing anger. I'm not an angry person but now I'm straining to keep it all in.

'Okay', he says. His voice is free of anger or frustration. I think of how patient he has been with my illness these past months. How he hits that mark of care and does not overreact at watching me disappear from myself for a moment. How lucky I am to have him, yet that fear in the pit of my stomach that I cannot push him too far. What if one day it's too much and he leaves? I would understand his decision, but still, the thought is unbearable. Later, I'll tell Mathew this and he will be appalled. It will take months of therapy for me to confront this internalised ableism.

He continues, 'Okay. Let's go.'

As quickly as the anger filled me up, it whooshes out. It's as though I'm holding onto a blown balloon, wrestling with it to tie a knot, and it drops from my grip, rushing across the room. I'm deflated. The seizures make me tired. If it's not the effects of recovery, it's feeling run down by constantly worrying about one happening. I realise that however angry I might be at how people perceive the seizures, I'm angrier that the episodes have become such a part of my life.

It's difficult for me not to slip into the line of thinking that with conversion there is a less serious risk of harm than epilepsy. I tell myself that it's understandable, given that Western medicine has been invested in the idea of mind–body dualism for centuries. And while the DSM-IV says that this dualism is 'a reductionist anachronism', it still governs the way medicine operates.

French philosopher Rene Descartes was probably the first to describe mind–body dualism, seeing the mind and brain as distinct from one another. The brain housed intelligence whereas the mind held consciousness, and presumably, what would later be called mental illness. British philosopher and psychologist Horace Romano Harré interprets Descartes, writing, 'While our bodies are all fashioned out of the same stuff, each individual mind is a unique "thinking thing", an ego identified with the soul.'

I read a study of mental health workers that shows that the majority think of illness in the ways shaped by their professions: it's either in the mind or brain. The study on schizophrenia found that participants, after the illness was framed as 'bio-genetic', felt a stigma towards those living with schizophrenia. Even more surprisingly, the majority of participants viewed the patient in 'less human terms' than when schizophrenia was viewed as without genetic cause and conceptualised as 'psycho-environmental'. The only thing more consistent, perhaps, than mind–body dualism is fear of illness.

Psychiatrist Joachim Raese agrees, writing in the *Journal of Psychiatry* that psychiatry's over-reliance on mind-body dualism affects the stigma of mental illness: 'Psychiatry has failed to effectively address the stigmatiza-tion of mental illness. This failure may be traced to lack of clarity about the fundamental issue facing the field, the mind/body dualism pervasive in our culture.'

Mind–body dualism, as Raese writes, is a 'funda-mental issue'. The same idea, too, has presented in the discussion of 'organic' versus 'non-organic' causes. If a person experiences seizures due to a brain injury – let's say they fainted and hit their head on a table – then their sei-zures would be 'organic'. If a neurologist was to determine that, in their view, my brain was functioning normally then my seizures would be 'non-organic'.

This is a confusing distinction, to say the least. Like body–mind dualism, terminology around 'organic' causes suggests that 'organic' is valid, as there is a physiological issue that can be found, whereas 'non-organic' is a symp-tom of the 'mind' and is thus less serious. The premise is based on separating mind from matter, something that is becoming not only more difficult to do but increasingly seen as the incorrect approach.

Despite the experience of my seizures being the same

– large, looming frightening things – I will be pushed into the hands of a psychiatrist (non-organic) or neurologist (organic) depending on whether a series of tests find anything concerning in my brain. As Raese writes, there has been an 'unfortunate divorce of psychiatry from neurology', which limits a neurologist's or psychiatrist's ability to help the patient alone.

Terminology that imposes different ways to distinguish mental from physical origins of illness is not new. In the early twentieth century, the terms in fashion when describing mental illness were 'functional' and 'organic'. Much like today, 'organic' was considered to be 'real', as the illness is based on physical causes; say, chemical imbalances in the brain. 'Functional' was used to describe patients experiencing manic-depressive illness, now known as bipolar disorder or schizophrenia. Medical professionals using the term 'functional' then implied that the opposite is true; that these illnesses were brought about through 'abnormal' reactions to life events. While this language was common at the time, both bipolar disorder and schizophrenia are currently thought to be caused by a combination of genetic and environmental factors.

The medical profession is quick to ascribe cause to illness as either physical or what they view as the somewhat flimsier emotional and 'maladaptive' causes. Despite being uncertain of the origins of illness, diagnoses and consequently people's lives are forced to respond to the rigid boundaries of medical thinking of their time. I find it concerning that there is a rush to draw lines in the sand between similar experiences of illness. Physician Josef Breuer's patient, Anna O, who fell ill in 1880, has since been thought not to have experienced hysteria but complex partial seizures alongside drug dependence, according to psychiatrist Alison Orr-Andrawes. There have been multiple modern medical opinions that differ on Anna's diagnosis, all of which say it was not conversion. But to me, Anna O's diagnosis is not important. As a patient myself, I believe it was the care she received that should be spoken of, particularly as it lacked in perseverance and compassion. I wonder what Mary Glover's experience of medicine would have been if her illness fit a little more neatly into the ideas of the time. If her experience was a little more 'organic', would she have been spared hours of 'trials' and prayers through which she seized?

I think of the words of novelist Madeleine Thien, who writes in *Dogs at the Perimeter* about the connection of mind and matter:

> The number of possible brain states exceeds the number of elementary particles in the universe. Maybe what exists beneath (tissue and bone and cells) and what exists above (ourselves, memory, love) can be reconciled and understood as one thing, maybe it is all the same, the mind is the brain, the mind is the soul, the soul is the brain, etc. But it's like watching a hand cut open another hand, remove the skin, and examine the tissue and bone. All it wants is to understand itself. The hand might become self-aware, but won't it be limited still?

I learn that scientific understanding is increasingly leading us to realise that not only consciousness but personal experience manifest physically. It's a lofty idea and one that is hard to process but it seems medicine is moving towards being able to map personal experiences and memories on a brain circuit, at least to some extent.

But as Thien writes, how we live and the way our brains work – whether functioning through illness or what we view as health – is not and may never be fully understood. I like to think that perhaps all parts of us are grounded in the body. When we cry, maybe it's not just falling tears that show the physicality of our emotion; perhaps our sadness is mapped out in our brains, too.

What if all mental illness, from conversion to generalised anxiety, is 'organic' and we just don't yet have the tools to understand the full complexity of the brain?

*

The results come two weeks later via a phone call.

'*Normal* EEG', the nurse says. 'No fluid, no haemorrhages, no enlargement.' The nurse speaks of parts of the brain I haven't yet read about – the names slipping out of my ear as soon as she speaks it.

'Normal?' I can't quite grip the words she's spoken. How could everything appear to be normal?

'Yes', she says.

I keep asking her questions – groping awkwardly for any odd brain activity. 'No signs of epilepsy? They thought I could have epilepsy.'

She just says 'normal' again and again.

But the seizures, I think. I have nothing else to ask and so I reluctantly say goodbye. I sit in the silence of my living room after the call. A man is outside my window, which opens out onto a city street. He's talking loudly on the phone and I look at the shape of his skull, the neatly clipped greys and browns of his hair as he stretches his body back, looking to the sky.

I immediately call the psychiatrist's rooms and am put on hold. A lullaby sings from my phone, a metallic sound. I ask if I can move up my appointment. I need the clarity of hearing her thoughts and a way to move forward.

'The psychiatrist is on leave,' the receptionist says.

I had forgotten and I hate how needy and broken that makes me look. I thank her and hang up.

I look across my living room and see an ant crawling out from the front door across the yellow-toned floorboards. I notice the crunch of dried leaves by the hat stand, collecting in a corner by the front door. I can no longer think about the seizures; my mind is taken up by the ant's journey and those browned leaves.

A neighbour sweeps the leaves each Saturday morning, hunched over in the street. Directly in front of our door is a pile of collected leaves. There's a clear line where her small-handled broom has stopped and I always smile when I see it. I like that pile of leaves. It's as though we're collecting the remains of each day, to be greeted by the cycle of growing and dying when I leave the house.

Above me on the wall is my CT scan. Mathew has

placed it in a frame. I thought it was self-obsessed for me to have a picture of my brain hanging in my own home but once it's on the wall, it becomes a part of the living space. I forget it's *my* brain and love the odd mix of shapes that blur together. I often find myself staring at the blues of the scan. They have come alive against the white background of the frame but I can't look at it now. It's a reminder of the 'normal' result I keep getting. I should be grateful to be told that my body is working well. That I don't have an illness that requires complex surgery with all of its accompanying risks. I am grateful, of course, but underneath it lies a feeling of absence.

When I tell Mathew the EEG results that afternoon, he hugs me tight.

'This is great,' he says and I can feel the vibration of his voice against my cheek. I feel as though something has been sucked out of me. Mum, too, is happy. She has dropped in after work. When she sees the slouch in my shoulders she asks, 'What's wrong?' and I can't tell her.

I didn't want the complications of epilepsy but this hurts too, even if I am being told again and again that I have the easier condition to manage. Maybe it's grief that what I'm experiencing is 'all in my head'. Or as Mum reminds me, a normal EEG doesn't mean much. I could still have epilepsy. Many people with epilepsy appear to have normal brain waves on an EEG. Or it could be, and could have always been, conversion. A normal EEG just places me on the path for more testing, more conversations where I struggle to articulate my exact experience in the brief and expensive window where I talk to a specialist. I thought by now I'd have more answers.

I sit in my living room and feel the pull and tug of epilepsy and conversion. The EEG results pull me towards conversion disorder, supported by the weight of the CT scan. But in this world of medical ambiguity – where answers turn out to hold more questions – nothing is clear. I'm left in the middle, caught adrift between two illnesses. Tired and hallucinating.

*

Strengthen me, O Lord, against that Goliath.

– *Mary Glover, written by Stephen Bradwell.*

III.

KATHARINA

I decide to lock myself away. It's to look after my brain, I say.
To lower the anxiety that lives at a high hum in my bones.
During this time, I don't do much. I write with my dog
beside me, feet twitching as she sleeps. I see my parents.
Go to work twice a week to make rent, thanking my mind
that a seizure has not yet occurred in front of students. If I
were religious, I would pray to anyone for this to continue.
And, most of all, I try to sleep at night. It's a stripped-down
existence but it is still whole. I begin to relax and feel the
ligaments and muscles unclench within me.

At some point, the message of healing rest becomes
lost and I begin to fear being outside. I worry that to be
present and fully engage – to take everything around me
in – will bring on a seizure. I morph from someone who is
sick to this meek thing. I try not to remember how I used
to be vibrant, a force out in the world. Where I once spoke
out, I am now quiet. I let Mathew speak for me while I look
down and examine my hands. For the first time, I notice a

small scar shaped like a 'T' on my right index finger. I take to looking at it when I become overwhelmed.

Through the seizures, I've noticed that my interior world has become increasingly compelling. And so, I think more than I speak. I am caught in a world I hadn't fully been aware of. The seizures have not gone away, they've only been dampened. Instead of big rushes of alien thoughts and shrinking walls, they have begun to integrate in small ways into my daily life. I look at faces and am amazed, caught in wonder at these things built from muscle and skin. It's as though I've only seen half a dozen people in my life. Each face is magical. The shapes catch my eye and I stare at everyone I pass.

My eyes fixate on the smallest details. I am struck by the way the light catches and beams off the red leather lounge in Mum's study. I stare at it while she speaks, her words drifting into me. I've been in this room with that same couch thousands of times – I would watch *The Simpsons* here as a child and then on to *The OC* and *Frasier* in my teen years. Only now, the shine of it catches me off-guard and I feel a sense of wonder.

I take up yoga again. Mathew surprises me with a gift of ten classes. We never give gifts – not for Christmas or the birthday we coincidentally share. He wants to help, I think. So when he tells me what he's done, I smile hard and try not to cry. In our first class, the yoga teacher tells us that the positions we fold ourselves into should not cause us pain. We stretch out on the floor and my foot brushes

Mathew's. He's warm and soft. He turns and smiles at me and I'm caught up in the kindness of him.

'No pain, no discomfort,' the instructor repeats over and over as her feet pad lightly around the room, watching us as we bend over ourselves.

I try to adopt this way of thinking. I whisper her words to myself, hoping they will drape over my own world like an incantation.

I leave the house.

No pain.

When I take a step, I can feel the harshness of the pavement thundering up my feet into my knees. I miss the softness of walking barefoot through my corridor, my garden.

No discomfort.

I'm in the car and watch the flickering, changing faces of people on the street. I see a white-haired man with long sideburns and am drawn in.

No pain.

My eyes fixate on the dotted grooves of a ceiling, reminding me of Lego bricks or a crumbling block of cheese. It hurts to pull my vision away.

No discomfort.

I now wonder what's worse: full seizures or drifting absently from one place to another? Like a ghost, I affect nothing. Only witness. I'm not sure if I'm healing or whether I'm becoming a fractured version of myself. I think again of the woman in the depersonalisation book, *Feeling Unreal.* I read her words, over and over:

Yet sometimes, I feel a little sorry for them, especially
when they're overly self-confident. They think they
know who they really are.

I wonder how I fit within this illness. Is recovery meant to
hurt or am I becoming sicker?

*

In his book *Studies on Hysteria*, co-authored with his
mentor, physician Josef Breuer, Freud meticulously writes
up the lives and treatments of five 'hysterical' patients.
Freud writes of a conversation he has with his fourth
patient, Katharina, a 'sulky-looking girl of perhaps eighteen', who approaches him during a summer holiday in the
late 1800s. Reading this, over 120 years later, I'm intrigued
to discover someone with a name so close to mine. I was
combing Freud's work for shared symptoms, but my disori-
ented brain wonders if Katharina was – is – somehow me.

Freud begins the chapter with himself: 'I made an
excursion into the Hohe Tauern so that for a while I might
forget medicine and more particularly the neuroses.' After
walking up a mountain ('a strenuous climb') he, 'feeling
refreshed and rested, was sitting deep in contemplation'.
Katharina comes to him as he sits in her family's 'refuge
hut', asking whether he is a doctor, then revealing, 'The
truth is, sir, my nerves are bad. I went to see a doctor ...
about them and he gave me something for them; but I'm
not well yet.'

In her words – and her meekness – I can sense Katharina's desperation. I've lived it; am living it. *Can you help me?* The phrase beats under the surface of every medical appointment. The answer, if I'm lucky, is 'maybe'. Worse is when they say 'yes' and fill you with medication that makes you sicker. I've grown wary of expensive offices and confidence that is louder than my own voice.

But when Katharina finds Freud, he does not think of her. He pities himself, his moment on a mountaintop lost to someone's illness. He writes: 'So there I was with the neuroses once again for nothing else could very well be the matter with this strong, well-built girl with her unhappy look.' But he looks at her with curiosity too. She is a spec-imen to him: 'I was interested to find that neuroses could flourish in this way at a height of over 6,000 feet.' I know the look of curiosity well, much as Katharina would have. It's difficult, knowing that someone sees you as a puzzle. Not quite human. Freud later writes after diagnosing Katharina with 'acquired hysteria' that 'this solved the riddle' and 'thus the case was cleared up' as if a 'case' was all Katharina was.

This was not the first time Freud was more interested in 'truth' than in treating the patient. In her book *In the Freud Archives*, journalist Janet Malcolm describes one of Freud's most famous cases, Dora. Malcolm writes that during Dora's analysis, where Freud asserted Dora was experiencing hysteria, he 'was more like a police inspector interrogating a suspect than like a doctor helping a patient'.

*

Psychogenic non-epileptic seizures are not static. While there might be no organic cause, they present differently in each patient and each stressor is as varied as the patients themselves. Professor of Neurology Ronald P Lesser writes for the American Epilepsy Society's *Epilepsy Currents* that the aetiologies of PNES are:

> Disturbance in patient interactions. This refers to patient interactions that are filled with conflict such as those by survivors of abuse or patients experiencing familial conflict;

> Internalised conflict, often brought about by patients who experience panic attacks, anxiety disorders, obsessive-compulsive disorder, dissociative disorder and PTSD;

> History of psychosis, like schizophrenia;

> Experience of personality disorders like borderline, narcissistic or avoidant personality disorder; or

> History of head trauma as shown through MRI and/ or EEG results.

'Internalised conflict' seems to describe me a little too well; it's discomforting. I tick the boxes, too, of anxiety disorders through OCD, panic attacks and generalised anxiety. As if those weren't enough to live with. But I worry that perhaps it was my inability to control them that sent me down this PNES path.

Lesser also writes while exploring the origins of PNES with a patient that: 'conversations alone are sufficient to allow control of PNES in some patients: two of nine patients in one series and three of 27 in another'. That feels magical to me. To know the *why* can disintegrate the symptoms as if they were never there to begin with. I am prone to self-reflection to an extreme degree, ticking over what I've said and done and *who* I am daily. To think my way through an illness feels revolutionary.

Yet I know this won't be the cure for me. I've been sitting on the 'why' of my seizures for months now. I am not certain but it seems likely they originated from a deep place of anxiety around books and success, which stand in for insecurities around worth and belonging. I am not anxious because I write; I am anxious because I don't know if I'm good enough, not as a writer but as a person. But dwelling on my need to fit, to have a purpose and nestle in beside a history of writers, as a book would on a shelf, has not cured me.

I'm sure I am in the majority of patients who require further treatment to control their seizures. But what that treatment could be is unclear. Lesser writes that, 'among the studies of treatment of PNES, no single strategy appears most effective'. Patients can receive in- or outpatient therapy, talk therapy or behavioural therapy as well as less-known therapies like biofeedback, meditation and relaxation therapy. There is little mention of medication in the treatment of PNES, although I'm sure there is no hesitance to prescribe. It seems, when it is used, medication is there to alleviate symptoms rather than stop the seizures.

These variations in treatment perplex me somewhat. Are the treatments tailored to a patient group whose circumstances and experience of PNES are nuanced? Or are physicians unsure of how to treat a seizure disorder that has no known organic basis – throwing therapies at patients and hoping one will stick? It's hard to say but overall, in the studies at least, treatment outcomes seem to be positive.

Out of six studies, 29–52 per cent of patients ceased to experience seizures after therapy, and 15–43 per cent had reduced instances of seizures. But a study by neurology professors Thomas Lempert and Dieter Schmidt shows that perhaps a reduction in seizures is not just up to the individual's progress in therapy. It seems that seizure control depends on the underlying psychiatric diagnosis. Out of 30 patients with existing psychiatric diagnoses, 23 did not become seizure-free while seven did. Patients experiencing PNES without another psychiatric diagnosis had drastically different results, with six patients experiencing no seizures while two continued to have episodes.

I'm scared to learn where I'll sit in these statistics. I'm not sure if I will be one of the lucky seven out of 30 who recover despite living with an additional psychiatric diagnosis. I wonder how useful statistics are for people like me.

Once again, they raise the questions: am I normal? Where do I fit?

*

Katharina describes the nature of her illness with such detail that my throat catches a little reading her words. Freud writes of their conversation:

> 'It comes over me all at once. First of all it's like something pressing on my eyes. My head gets so heavy, there's a dreadful buzzing, and I feel so giddy that I almost fall over. Then there's something crushing my chest so that I can't get my breath.'

> 'And you don't notice anything in your throat?'

> 'My throat's squeezed together as though I were going to choke.'

> 'Does anything else happen in your head?'

> 'Yes, there's a hammering, enough to burst it.'

> 'And don't you feel at all frightened while this is going on?'

> 'I always think I'm going to die. I'm brave as a rule and go about everywhere by myself into the cellar

and all over the mountain. But on a day when that
happens I don't dare to go anywhere; I think all the
time someone's standing behind me and going to
catch hold of me all at once.'

I wonder what it means for her that she doesn't 'dare to
go anywhere'. I can't help but imagine the pain she feels
at her movements being so restricted and how this twists
her own self-perception in knots. I too was once 'brave as
a rule'.

*

Graphic novelist David B writes in his memoir *Epileptic* of
his brother's illness that, 'It looks like he's pausing on the
frontier between the two worlds'. Seeing David B's drawings of his brother, eyes unfocused, drool falling down his
chin, is confronting, challenging the reader to look at what
epilepsy is.

Like David B's brother, I feel caught between two
worlds. Struggling between presence and absence; living
and dying; breathing and swallowing. I am either myself
or lost within my own body, trapped through anxiety and
worry.

I feel this all the more keenly after going with Mathew
and two new friends to a performance that mimics a séance.
I'm nervous, both for what the séance could bring as well
as navigating a social interaction with new people. The
four of us, along with the rest of the audience, are locked

in a shipping container for twenty minutes in complete darkness. We sit in old red velvet cinema seats, ears covered by noise-cancelling headphones, and the show begins. To summon the 'ghosts', we are asked to place our hands on the table. Voices whisper around me, filtering in from the headphones. I feel the table shake as a man jumps onto it, pacing back and forth. He bends forward, whispering into the face of the person two to my left: 'Why are you here?'

I know it's not real. The noises around me come from a recording. But my palms, which are face down on the table, register the thump of feet. I can hear a voice grow and swell as it moves around the room. I am in darkness but wonder, if I reached out, would I touch a man's shins?

Sitting in the darkness, I begin to see white blots. They shift, beginning in my left eye's peripheral vision and then moving down to my knees. The blotches shimmer and move, like a drop of water falling into a full glass. I take them in, knowing that they, like the voices playing in my headset, are not real.

How different is this to what I see during a seizure? In a seizure, my mind produces sensations and here, the show's creators evoke them. Yet there is a similarity I can't quite place. During an episode, I look at my hands over and over. They gauge my progress. When they begin to seem familiar again, I feel safe. The urge to reach out is strong. I rub my fingers over each other, pinching flesh as I go. I feel their boniness and am grounded in this dark room.

It is not real, but I am.

*

I think I began writing this book to make sense of what was happening. To understand what it means when your mind unfurls and twists itself into knots you can no longer recognise. Along the way, I had hoped that understanding would illuminate a pathway to health. But the more I learn about the complexities and the lack of knowledge around conversion, the more my hope dwindles.

Memoirist Sian Prior writes in the magazine *Dumbo Feather* on her book *Shy* that, 'My secret hope – that writing a memoir about shyness would cure me of my shyness – was never realised. I could not re-build my personality with words. What I did, though, was cure myself of the desire to be someone else.'

Perhaps Prior's ending, for me, would be enough. Acceptance of who I am, seizures and all, could be my happy conclusion. Right now, though, it seems so far away. I'm not sure if I can settle for this as my life. An everyday of distorted shapes and fixed gazes. Not knowing if my experience of the world reflects the reality of those around me. We're so often told to fight an illness, as if all illness were something we could conquer if we tried hard enough. I'm caught between wanting to fight it and knowing that isn't possible. I want to be free of it but within me, I dread knowing that all that I have power to do is accept it.

In *The Shaking Woman*, Siri Hustvedt found out her convulsions were, after all, something familiar. They were not conversion disorder, but part of the migraines she had experienced throughout her life. She writes on accepting this new part of herself: 'Perhaps because she was a late arrival, I have had a much harder time integrating the shaking woman but as she becomes familiar, she is moving out of the third person and into the first.'

The seizures are a late arrival. I've lived with anxiety and OCD for more years than I haven't. I know their ins and outs. Although they are always in flux – like memories, an intrusive thought can morph and change over years – we have a familiar rapport. The seizures are an unknown. They have rushed into my life and firmly stayed over the past ten months. I don't know when or if they'll ever leave.

The seizures are a new addition but, perhaps unlike anxiety and OCD, could be a useful one, in a way. PNES is said to be a self-protective measure. Could this be true? I imagine them as black-caped figures, swooping in to protect me from crowded supermarkets and rejection slips. They take me away, as best as they can. The seizures are painful to live through but maybe they're protecting me from something worse.

Neurologist Suzanne O'Sullivan writes about a patient she calls Camilla in her book of somatic illness, *It's All in Your Head*. Camilla lives with psychogenic non-epileptic seizures, or as O'Sullivan prefers to call them, 'dissociative seizures'. Camilla's seizures are similar to 'grand mal' epilepsy in that she shakes and convulses. However, when the specialists can find no organic cause, O'Sullivan believes the seizures to be psychosomatic. She thinks that they are due to anxiety and guilt over the death of Camilla's first child, whose pram was hit by an oncoming car when she looked away and lost her grip for a moment.

O'Sullivan says: 'Camilla had consigned her pain to a place in her brain that she could not fully access. She knew that she had lost a son but she had forgotten the pain of it. Her pain was locked in a box in her head. The seizures were the monster that protected that box. They were her monster and they served a purpose, and only when their secret was revealed did the seizures disappear.'

I can understand the box in Camilla's head. Losing a child because of an absentminded moment where she let go and the pram rolled away onto the street – that monster is unbearable. To lock it away seems natural.

Myself, I understand less. How could anything be locked away in my head that is so hard to face that I experience seizures? Unlike a third of women who experience PNES, I did not experience a significant traumatic event before the onset of my illness. I've always considered my traumas as a pain of an everyday variety, experienced by others. It took a long time to unlearn this but at first, I felt as though the cumulative traumas of my life didn't count.

As poet Meera Atkinson writes in *Traumata*, 'I did what many people so often do – I thought in terms of a hierarchy of suffering, concluding I had no right to be as affected as I was.' Reviewer Jocelyn Hungerford expands on this idea in the essay 'Women Who Write About Their Feelings and Lives' for the *Sydney Review of Books*: 'It is, I've learned, symptomatic of trauma to believe you don't deserve help because others have suffered worse. This is a zero-sum view of compassion and it's infectious'.

My past experiences – whether violent words from men's lips or watching someone I love suffer a painful death – did not fit within my conceptualised 'hierarchy of suffering'. And so, reading study upon study on PNES, I pushed away the possibility of trauma being the seed of my illness; at the time, I was not ready to confront the slippery nature of trauma rather than my own rigid definition.

At times, I have wondered, quickly and foolishly, if the seizures occur because of a repressed memory. Reading Freud, it was hard to avoid the idea of a past memory living underneath the surface. The possibility of repressed abuse crept into my consciousness; but I knew it could not be so. Fully repressed memories are not common. While trauma can blur memories, rarely does it erase them completely. I was looking for an answer where there was none. In no way was I hoping to remember abuse, but I hoped for the clarity of an answer, one that I am beginning to learn might not be available.

So for some of us, perhaps the trigger may not be a single traumatic event but instead a slow build of everyday aggressions. Perhaps these traumas cumulate, flooding over to somatic manifestations.

I remember thinking I had tinnitus as a child. When I practised the violin, filling the house with a laboured, crunchy version of 'Eleanor Rigby', I would hear the sound of bells ringing in the distance. Often, it would become such a distraction that I would stop playing, in the hope of catching the ringing noise. It sounded like the pull of

Santa's sleigh and only came to me when I practised. Perhaps this too was a form of conversion. I hated the violin. I loathed how slowly learning to play came for me and the way my neck would sweat as I clasped the wooden instrument to my chin. Once I confessed to my parents that I had no love for playing music and quit the stilted weekly violin lessons, the ringing stopped and has never returned.

Reading Camilla's story, I realise that it is not the first I have come across that shares aspects of my own illness. I find myself reading case studies compulsively. Reading about illness is such a comfort. Seeing my symptoms and experiences reflected back to me assures me I am not alone. I am not irreparably broken as I fear, but share an experience with another person. Feeling our lives connect through illness eases the tightness in my chest.

I begin to hope that I'll read my own story, word for word, in someone else. To read this her–me (conversion patients are predominantly women) would be to have it clearly laid out in front of me. I would know how to vanquish the seizures. It, or rather I, would be solved. If only I could find her, I could find a way to end the confusion. No more tests, or doubt. I'd know.

Yet I haven't found a story that shares much with my own and I'm not sure I ever will. Perhaps because stories of psychosomatic illness aren't told or maybe, I dread to think, no one else's is quite like mine. My seizures are alive and unique, no matter how much I wish the opposite to be true.

*

As well as being unable to breathe, Katharina would often see 'an awful face that looks at me in a dreadful way, so that I'm frightened'. After hearing her symptoms, Freud thought to himself: 'Was I to make an attempt at an analysis? ... I should have to try a lucky guess.'

Freud 'guesses' that Katharina 'must have seen or heard something that very much embarrassed you, and that you'd much rather not have'. Katharina agrees, telling him of discovering her uncle sexually abusing her cousin; the uncle had also attempted to assault Katharina on multiple occasions. Upon hearing this, Freud suggests that the 'awful face' Katharina saw was in fact her uncle. At first, she disagrees, but then realises he is correct (although Freud might well have pushed her in this direction). In Freud's recounting, Katharina says:

> Yes, I know now. The head is my uncle's head I
> recognize it now but not from that time. Later, when
> all the disputes had broken out, my uncle gave way
> to a senseless rage against me. He kept saying that
> it was all my fault: if I hadn't chattered, it would
> never have come to a divorce [with my aunt]. He
> kept threatening he would do something to me; and
> if he caught sight of me at a distance his face would
> get distorted with rage and he would make for me
> with his hand raised. I always ran away from him,

and always felt terrified that he would catch me some time unawares. The face I always see now is his face when he was in a rage.

I wonder if realising this would have been enough to make Katharina's attacks go away. Or once Freud left, did she spin out without someone to talk to about the traumatic circumstances of her early life?

Pioneering psychoanalyst Pierre Janet and Freud both believed that telling was what made the difference in trauma. Janet focuses on the trauma of potential injury, describing a thirty-eight-year-old patient who, confronted by the experience of almost developing a vision impairment, cannot bear the shock of it. He cannot see, unable to look at what has happened (or nearly happened) to him. By contrast, Freud writes of patients who are traumatised by experiences of abuse, like Katharina. Freud digs these experiences out – perhaps despite what the patient is prepared for in the moment – and brings them from past memories to the present.

Freud says after writing about Katharina, 'I hope this girl, whose sexual sensibility had been injured at such an early age, derived some benefit from our conversation. I have not seen her.' In the search for understanding, it seems, patients are often left behind. They become case studies to be pondered. Later, when Freud claimed that traumatic memories were often fabricated, I imagine his patients felt this betrayal all too keenly. Freud never saw Katharina again; he can never have known whether his two-hour 'therapy' session on a mountaintop was beneficial or not.

Josef Breuer's patient 'Anna O', who is now known to be Bertha Pappenheim, was one of the most famous 'hysterical' patients who was – much like Katharina – eventually left behind. When her therapeutic relationship with Breuer ended, she became sicker and was subsequently institutionalised. At this, 'Breuer told Freud that she was deranged; he hoped she would die to end her suffering'.

Yet Bertha went on. She contributed to women's lives for the better through her engagement with social work. In 1904, twenty-two years after her therapy with Breuer, Bertha founded the League of Jewish Women. The league was one of the leading forces of the Jewish feminist movement in Germany and, like other feminist organisations Bertha developed, it was led by and consisted only of women. Bertha wrote compellingly of her experience as a girl:

> This can already be seen in the different reception
> given a new citizen of the world. If the father or
> someone else asked what 'it' was after a successful
> birth, the answer might be either the satisfied report
> of a boy, or – with pronounced sympathy for the
> disappointment – 'Nothing, a girl,' or 'Only a girl'.

Bertha was an incredible woman who actively built organisations that improved the lives of other women and girls. But despite her achievements, unfortunately she is mostly remembered for her illness. Like Katharina, Bertha was a patient – Breuer's patient – and not her own person.

But the saddest part, perhaps, to me is what Suzanne O'Sullivan writes in *It's All in Your Head*: '… for all the shortcomings in the concepts proposed by Freud and Breuer in *Studies*, the 21st century has brought no great advances to a better understanding of the mechanisms for this disorder.' Reading this, I'm filled with fear. I wonder if criticising Freud and Breuer and the way they used patients to build diagnostic frameworks means I am criticising the only tools I have. But after discovering psychiatrist and researcher Judith Herman's *Trauma and Recovery*, my thoughts start to shift. She writes that 'Denial, repression, and dissociation operate on a social as well as an individual level.' Collectively, we repress, deny and dissociate from trauma. I think we forget the women who came before us who experienced illness a lot like mine. While there might not be greater diagnostic knowledge, according to O'Sullivan, there are years of women's lives that address navigating this illness. Herman later writes: 'Survivors challenge us to reconnect fragments, to reconstruct history, to make meaning of their present symptoms in light of past events.' The women I read – Edith, Mary, Katharina – challenge me to reconnect my own fragments. To make my own meaning of this illness.

*

While the seizures grow less severe as I lock myself away, they become increasingly frequent. I have a seizure alone at a café. I'm sitting outside, my forearms brushing a weather-worn wooden table as I type on my laptop. I begin to feel myself float away. Or perhaps it's more accurate to say I shrink down into a small figurine, buried within myself.

I try to move my hands but they stay still. I keep willing them to move, not used to having to concentrate so hard to move a limb. Nothing feels natural. Eventually, I manage to wrap my hand around the paper coffee cup. During seizures, I cannot taste anything and I hope to measure how bad it is using the intensity of bitter liquid on my tongue. I put the coffee to my lips, swishing it back and forth over my tastebuds. I can taste it, just, and I allow myself to sink into the chair, feeling relief. My hand still rests around the coffee cup and I feel its warmth pulsate out on to my skin. It's a comfort and I rest for a moment, my vision fixating on the creased linen shirt of a woman nearby. My hand becomes hotter and hotter and I can feel a burning sensation as it stays looped around the coffee cup. I will it to move but it remains, still and burning. Slowly, using the kind of intense effort I'd use doing a last set of weights (when I was well enough to spend an hour on such a feat), I pull my hand away by a centimetre or two until the heat no longer seeps into the soft skin of my palm. My eyes move to my hand and the palm is pink. I try to look away, settling on the 'T' scar on my index finger to calm me while I wait for this to pass.

The next day, I have a seizure during yoga class. I manage to time it, looking at the large white clock nailed to the wall. For fifteen minutes, I beg my body to move as instructed while light shimmers and my vision tunnels in on a scuff mark on the wall. The black lines remind me of a highway at night, constantly in motion.

Later that night, Mathew says I hid the seizure well – he didn't know what was happening a metre from his own yoga mat – but in the mirrored yoga studio I could see myself unravel fully. It's disconcerting watching myself as the illness descends. My face is set in blankness, as in sleep when all the muscles grow slack. I look soulless and seeing that reflected back at me frightens me. My eyes are small and hollow and I wonder why no one has come up to ask me, 'What is wrong with you?'

That night, I cannot sleep. I keep thinking of myself as the woman with the hollow, shrunken eyes. My feet rub together and tap at an invisible wall. Mathew groans, 'Stop twitching.' I try to hold myself still while the thoughts rush. My body feels alive, each muscle hot with nerves.

Before I only knew what a seizure felt like, but seeing it painted on my face has scared me. I knew what it was to feel removed but to see myself as an absence feels beyond what I can handle. Even though I was living with illness, I hadn't imagined how frightening it would look worn on my face.

*

When I first went on the antidepressants, I was struck by their effect on my attention span. Still studying law, I would sit in a lecture theatre, rapt at the words flowing through me. My eyes fixed on the lecturer, taking everything in fully. I didn't take notes; I didn't need to. The discussions on the permissibility of evidence filled me up.

I'm not sure if it was the medication that did this, or the fact I was so nauseous I wasn't eating. Perhaps it was the hunger, living underneath the intense nausea, that made me listen so eagerly. Maybe an animal part of me thrived on the sharp fear hunger evokes in the body. I thought – or maybe hoped – that this intense ability to concentrate was how I would always feel from now on. I would absorb information fully, be able to sit through a two-hour lecture without fading. Of course, this was not the case. Like the nausea, it lasted a week or so before I returned to normalcy. But for a moment, I had a window into a different life with a changed brain.

In a way, this rapture is back, although it's not a lecturer's words I fixate on but faces. My fascination with them continues to tinge my life. At the market, I watch a woman with faded tattoos stretching up her arms to grasp a tomato and bring it to her nose, inhaling deeply.

The joy in observing people, I think, is that I can live outside of myself. I am caught up in their lives, pushed away with them as if following a river's current. I sit with Mathew and am too busy following the lives of the people around us to focus on his words. I don't want to stare – to be taken out of my own life only to be amazed at those passing me by – but I am. When I see them, I don't think. My mind is still as I take everything in. It's as though I'm a blank canvas and each person I see places a brushstroke of colour onto me.

Three weeks later, I dream that I'm in hell. Unlike most dreams, this stays with me and I catch my mind falling back into that world in idle moments. In the dream, I live in hell with a drone of others. We have had the emotions stripped out of us and exist as shells. It is part of some grand plan and I am unable to feel.

Hell, I learn in my dreams, is a never-ending creaking house with narrow doors I have to shimmy through. It is a public bathroom with low-doored stalls where everyone can watch one another, the smell of piss permeating the room. It is a supermarket aisle with bundles of vintage clothes too small for my body hanging in clusters from the shelves. It is a theatre I enter fifteen minutes late and everyone – even those on stage – pausing to turn and look at me. I live in these places for weeks in my dream world and slowly notice that, unlike the drones I'm surrounded by, my emotions start to come back. It's as though that invisible spell that has been cast on all of us has started to fail. I fall in love with the Devil and he me. He takes the form of actor Ted Danson from *The Good Place* and we kiss and fuck in the supermarket aisles.

Ted Danson has to leave (there is work to do in hell, he tells me) and I am left on my own, wandering with the flock of the mindless. I have to hide the feelings, even though they become keener as the days pass. I know that if

I am caught, it will be the end. To feel is to be punished in this world my mind has constructed.

When I am alone, I circle the aisles and tears drip down my face. They are heavy and marked black with mascara. I know what will happen to me if others see that I can feel but the tears will not stop. I try to hide, ducking between aisles and burying my face in rows of lube and panty liners. But I am seen. Slowly, more people gather around me. When they see the tears, their eyes spread wide and fingers point outstretched. They are still, as if my dream has been paused and they live as images not people. They stay unmoving and I feel sick with fear.

I wake, the fear still in my throat. I stretch my legs out underneath the cool linen quilt. Freud said, on interpreting dreams, that 'deeper research will one day trace the path further and discover an organic basis for the mental event'. But I don't think it takes a psychoanalyst to understand my dream. To be ill in the obvious way a seizure brings is to be seen in a way that hurts. I am out of sync with the world and feel watched; ostracised.

*

Freud gives ten pages to Katharina's story of illness. I'm caught by how he writes her; her words are written as they were 'impressed on' Freud's memory but, to me at least, they do not read true. When Freud suggests Katharina saw something she did not wish to see, she replies, 'Heavens, yes!' and then, after he asks her for further details, 'You can say anything to a doctor, I suppose.' Katharina, despite the trauma she has lived through and her eighteen years of life, feels *too* young. He writes her as though she is naïve – something I find hard to believe knowing that she approached Freud after reading his name in the visitors' book of her aunt's 'refuge hut'. She is bolder – and smarter – than Freud credits her.

Part of me wonders whether Freud shaped this woman's story into a counterpoint to his more urban patients. After probing into her story of assault by her uncle, he (somewhat creepily) asks: 'What part of his body was it that you felt that night?' She makes no reply and Freud writes:

> She smiled in an embarrassed way, as though she had been found out, like someone who is obliged to admit that a fundamental position has been reached where there is not much more to be said. I could imagine what the tactile sensation was which she had later learnt to interpret. Her facial expression seemed to me to be saying that she supposed that I was right in my conjecture.

He no longer writes her as a child but gives her a coy, sexual sensibility that seems implausible given the circumstances. Freud contrasts her story – one that seems to resolve itself after a single conversation – with his other patients. 'In any case I owed [Katharina] a debt of gratitude for having made it so much easier for me to talk to her than to the prudish ladies of my city practice, who regard whatever is natural as shameful.' It's as though Freud is blaming his patients for not being more open, as if this alone is what is preventing a 'cure'.

In infantilising then sexualising Katharina, Freud has turned her into the ideal patient. One who agrees with him; gives him what he needs. And as a reward, only then, may she be 'cured'. Freud leaves Katharina and 'she was like someone transformed. The sulky, unhappy face had grown lively, her eyes were bright, she was lightened and exalted.'

Reading these ten pages, I worry that I am moving further from understanding Katharina. With each detail I am given, I question Freud. I wonder whether Freud was capable of writing her as she was, and not who he hoped her to be.

*

At Adelaide Writers' Week, I listen to writer and theologian Sarah Sentilles speak. She says that the belief that we can move past life's confusion – the 'thicket', she calls it – is misguided. Life is the experience of grappling. We are not given resolution, but have to continue while questioning. It is hard to come to terms with the idea that I might never fully know the why of the seizures, or if I'll be able to work through them. If stopping them is even possible. Like David B's brother I am stuck, living and grappling, between two worlds.

In *Shy*, Sian Prior recounts her experience with what I believe to be conversion disorder and how she overcame it. Prior was backpacking for six months during her youth and found that being alone and travelling, not speaking for weeks, had created a lump in her throat. 'At first', she writes, 'I thought there was something stuck down there, a crumb of bread crust or a tiny olive pip.' But then Prior realises that the lump swells or shrinks depending on her actions. If she communicates with others, it shrinks but as her loneliness and isolation grows, so does the lump. It disappears when she returns home. She writes of the moment she felt it leave her, starting a new job where she makes a speech in front of a crowd of 20 000 people on behalf of the Australian Conservation Foundation. She is free of the lump but, perhaps, not completely free of its cause. Throughout the book, Prior continues to question and grapple with her shyness. It is an affliction that she cannot seem to move past even though the lump is long gone.

I would give anything to melt away the seizures through a grand symbolic act. But maybe I wouldn't feel relief. Maybe, instead, I would focus on the next illness. If there were no seizures, I wonder if I would spend my days trying to deconstruct the next thing. If the seizures stop occupying my thoughts, perhaps I will fall into thinking through the familiar illness of panic attacks or obsessive thoughts.

Maybe, for me, there will be no happy ending or peace. I will just hop from one disorder to another.

*

I tell Mum about Katharina and the coincidence of our not quite but almost shared identity. She looks at me, confused. 'But it is your name.'

I say nothing, trying to catch a hint of uncertainty in her tone but there is none.

'It's German. Katherine and all its forms are from the Greek, Katerina.'

How had I not pieced this together? I want to yell back, ashamed of my ignorance. After my frustration settles, it seems so obvious. Mum always told me when I was little that I was named after my grandmothers – my German grandmother, Katherine and my Yiayia, Maria. My name, like me, ended up more Greek than German.

But while our name ties us in one way, I know we are deeply different. I live with a power Katharina did not have and she continues to lack agency in the way her illness has been told. Katharina's section in *Studies on Hysteria* is the shortest; after publication Freud said that her case history was not clinically valid. Katharina exists outside of medicine. She lives in a place that's been described as resembling a short story (by literary scholar John Ireland) and 'has attracted almost no critical consideration'. Ireland later notes that Katharina happened to come at the perfect time for Freud:

Katharina is the perfect remedy to the professional problems Freud mentions quite explicitly in the

opening sentences of his study: as a case history,
'Katharina' provides strong evidence in support of
Freud's controversial and as yet unproven theory
concerning the sexual etiology of hysteria.

Katharina is a remedy; she is a short story; she is Freud's
Case 4. She is strong, but she is not powerful. All that is
left of her is on the page and she wrote none of it. They are
Freud's words. Katharina's words are only recollections,
not fully her own. French feminist writer Hélène Cixous
might as well have meant Katharina when she writes that
'by writing her self, woman will return to the body which
has been more than confiscated from her, which has been
turned into the uncanny stranger on display'.

And in this, I realise that Katharina is not just a reflection of me – a woman who shares my name and an illness
– but an image of my great fear. One greater than seizures
pulsing through me each day. A fear that leaves me as just
an idea of hysteria.

Not a body, not a person but a case number to be read
and considered.

*

It takes weeks to see the psychiatrist after the EEG results
and I count each day until I'm there, as if I were a child
awaiting Christmas. But when it comes, I'm filled with the
fierce hum of nerves. I feel sick with it. I wanted answers and
was scared both that I would get them and that I wouldn't.

I walk into the dim light of the psychiatrist's room. Her hair is pulled back and her skin has a brown glow. Her skirt's peplum bursts out in blue at her hips. She looks comfortable, as if she is easing back into herself after her holiday.

As I fall into the familiar drop of the spongy leather seat, I feel uncomfortable that I haven't had time to put on make-up or brush the grey and white dog hair off my jeans. Usually I smear make-up on thick before a session. I don't want to look ill but today, I was too tired to walk myself through the pretence.

The psychiatrist looks through her files. 'The CT scan was clear.'

'And the EEG,' I chime in.

Her pen scrawls across her plain lined notepad. I listen to the clock tick, loud and concrete.

'And how is the sodium valproate?'

This is the question I've been dreading. I pause.

'It felt like death, so I stopped.'

She nods. 'Okay. I would have taken you off them today, anyway.'

A quick burst of fire expands in my chest. Living through the valproate – the falling asleep in public places and feeling of being already dead – was unnecessary after all. I push the thought aside, focusing on what the EEG means. I know that because the EEG is clear, it is increasingly unlikely the episodes are caused by epilepsy. Yet still, the psychiatrist asks me to go to a neurologist to confirm my suspicion. I'm reticent; more money, more tests.

Another specialist – a neurologist no less, whose profession shies away from psychosomatic illness. I dread explaining the nature of my episodes yet again and being met with curiosity. But I tell the psychiatrist, 'Yes, I'll go'.

'So, how have you been feeling?'

I tell her the story of the past four weeks. 'The world has become weightless, as if there is no bulk. At work, I see a row of shining black poles overlooking the garden as I eat my packed lunch. They look almost two-dimensional. I feel sure that if I were to reach out, I could not touch them.'

I pause to see her reaction but she is nodding along as I speak, eyebrows curved up in sympathy.

'It's like my hand would move through the pole. Like the world around me is a ghost.'

I go on, telling her the moment where I wasn't sure if I was dead or alive. An uncertainty that – if I wasn't so removed from my own body – would have shaken me to the core. Instead, in the mirrored yoga studio, I tried to rationally decide if I was experiencing life or death.

I watch my hands move about as I speak, expressing themselves in the Greek way of my childhood. I remember watching the women – my mother, my aunt and Yiayia – talking quickly, shifting from Greek to English depending on how appropriate their conversation was for a child's ears.

I hear the psychiatrist sigh in sympathy or perhaps it's a murmur. I look up to see the pity in her dark brown eyes. It gives me pause; I stop talking abruptly. I've run out of steam, talking about living with a sense of unreality. I'm too anxious, waiting to hear what she says. The uncertainty around my diagnosis feels too much to bear.

She begins to speak. 'I want to be clear: you're not psychotic. But from what you've described, you're bordering on psychosis.'

I say nothing. There is no air inside of me. I didn't know that psychosis was an option in the endless list of what is wrong with me. Adding conversion disorder already felt like too much; edging towards psychosis might be my breaking point.

'How would you feel about going on anti-psychotics?'

I know I must speak. I need to reply but I can't grasp at what to say.

'I ... I don't know.'

She explains what the meds will do but I'm not quite there as she speaks. It's as though a key part of me has walked out of the room, down the hall and through the heavy front door. I imagine sitting at the bakery across the street instead of being here, in this dim room. The psychiatrist gets up, leaving the room for a moment to get some sample medication while I am left awash with uncertainty.

It's later, after the session, that I realise being told you're not psychotic isn't a comfort, in one way. I'm 'bordering on psychosis', as if it were a state line I was entertaining crossing. I'm twenty-four years old and live in a land in between. I am not psychotic but I'm not fully here, in this world, either.

The psychiatrist passes me the meds. Two small packets.

I read the name, which sounds like a medical version of 'surfing'; as if taking anti-psychotics was a soothing ride or an exploration of the internet. This is not the answer I was hoping for. I was looking for clarity, not more complications and medications to take.

'Taking these will boost the effect of the anti-depressants', she says.

'O-kaay,' I say slowly, hoping to steer the conversation back to the EEG and the possibility of conversion. 'But let's say the neurologist says this is psychiatric not neurological. What ... what am I experiencing? I feel like I need something solid ... a diagnosis.'

The psychiatrist leans forward. Her chair is hard and stable and I resent the sinking trap of my leather armchair. I am not sure the psychiatrist will answer me clearly – nothing has been clear in this process – but perhaps she can sense I need some answers to move forward.

'Then I would say it's pseudoseizures brought on by extreme anxiety.'

I nod, relieved. Each time I've come here, I've heard something that has twisted the way I perceive myself. It seems as though I'm always shocked. At least this answer has not changed.

'And ... besides medication, what do we do?'

'Assertive stress management.' As she speaks, she clicks at the 'assertive' and it feels like seeing a bus come after a long wait. I laughed at the sass of her as she spoke. I liked the word – assertive. It meant business.

She continues, 'No relaxation techniques. No "maybe

this will help, maybe not". This will be getting in there, to the root.'

I nod and remember going to a psychologist years ago and being handed a worksheet to fill out. A table of fears, I think it was. It hadn't helped to write them down. It hadn't helped to sit in an expanse of quiet with a woman behind a desk. It hadn't helped to listen to her tell me what I already knew – that I was anxious.

'And I think you travelling to Europe is a test. It may help to be removed from your everyday. If while you're there the episodes decrease, there is your answer.'

As we'd walked to her office, I had told the psychiatrist I was leaving the next week to travel with Mum. She's going for work and I'm following. Two months before, it looked as though Mum needed a sudden hysterectomy due to a cancerous tumour. She wouldn't have recovered in time to get on the plane. For a reason neither Mum nor I have quite grasped, the tumour was benign and we're left with a trip together and the knowledge that our lives could have become something irrevocably different. The trip feels like the biggest gift we've ever received.

But now, it hurts that the trip has become a test – a litmus paper for how fucked up I am. It was supposed to be born out of joy, celebrating a rare instance in which cancer has not, once again, visited our family.

The psychiatrist looks at her watch, a small square face. It's time for me to go. She has checked it three times across the thirty-minute session, as well as pausing to take a call from Adelaide's largest psych ward. I suppose I understand; it's nearing four-thirty in the afternoon. These sessions with me do not have an overwhelming impact on her life, unlike the impact they have on mine. I leave, walking behind her wedged heels as they indent the carpet. My pace is more sedate than hers. Every part of me is slow and I struggle to keep up.

At the front desk, I pay an amount I can't afford and the words 'bordering on psychosis' run in circles through my mind. The 'surfing' anti-psychotics sit at the bottom of my bag by my copy of *Mrs Dalloway* – a book that has the tinge of hysteria. Woolf's character Septimus Warren experiences hysteria after returning from the war. In Woolf's time, Septimus's illness was known as shell shock: a diagnosis that psychiatry has argued would now be classified either as PTSD or conversion disorder. Like me, Septimus lives 'behind a pane of glass' and what makes him human – touch, taste, connection – has left him.

My slow, thick mind treads through these connections as I leave the office. The meds wait, crisp and unopened in their blister pack.

IV.
BLANCHE

The woman's face is blank, which makes me smile. Perhaps it's a visual pun, as her name is Blanche, which translates from the French to 'white' or 'blank'. Blanche Wittmann was known not by name but as the 'Queen of Hysterics'. It is hard to tell whether her expression is serene because in that moment she feels calm, or because she has slipped into her own oblivion. While Blanche's limp, undressed body and the men that surround her create a sense of gravity in André Brouillet's painting, it is the curve of her seizing, twisted hand which captures my eye. It points back at the nurses gathering behind her and away from the watching men. It declares, to me at least, 'I am ill. I am a hysteric.'

The painting was created in 1887 to capture neurologist Jean Charcot's Tuesday sessions – a public showing of hysterical women. It's large, almost life-sized, measuring nearly three by four metres. In it, a room of men seated in wooden chairs and crowding at the back watch Blanche collapse into the arms of another man, a doctor. Her head grazes his chest as her body hangs loosely, anchored upright only by his hands, which are hooked under her underarms. Her dress bunches at the waist; her top has been removed and her corset is showing. Her exposed shoulders gleam. To Blanche's right is Charcot in a black suit with matching black bow tie. His grey hair is slick and he stands resolutely. One hand is thrust out like Blanche's but unlike hers, his wrist is not twisted. He gestures to his audience as if he were emphasising an especially profound point.

In 1887, the painting was shown in Gallery 23 of the Salon in the Palais de l'Industrie, where it was viewed by over half a million people. Freud kept his own print in his office. And so I follow it to Paris. I learn that the painting, taller than I am, hangs flat against the wall, unframed, at the Musée d'Histoire de la Médecine on Boulevard Saint-Germain.

I walk the hour to the museum, down the Avenue des Champs-Élysées to the Place de la Concorde and across the Seine on to Boulevard Saint-Germain. The air is cold and sweet and my ears ache. As I approach Descartes University, a woman speaks to me in French and I feel as though I have passed. I apologise to her, in English, and she laughs and tells me in a strong British accent that she is not a Parisian either.

As I walk into the university's medical school, I hear the echo of footsteps reverberating through the wide hall. I am surrounded by white busts lining the room. It feels so different from other universities I've visited, and where I've studied. The building dates back to the Faculty of Medicine's establishment in 1806 and features marble and cool stone walls. I'm used to worn carpet and scratched wooden tables lingering from the 1970s. This is another world.

I walk up the aged steep wooden steps, gripping the railing tight. I hear the chatter of students, indistinct as I grasp only small clips of French. I stop halfway up the second flight to look at a painting of a woman dying of tuberculosis. It's also large and I'm absorbed by the detail of the needle entering the woman's arm as she is caught in a moment of pain and writhing. I think of the painting as I walk up the stairs – so many stairs – my heart beating. I can't tell if this is from excitement at seeing Brouillet's painting or physical exertion.

I reach the top of the landing. Before me is a wooden door with a sign announcing it is the medical museum. There is only a blank white wall beside it. The paint appears slightly faded next to the rich glossy staircase with worn wood marking a track up its centre. I walk into the museum hoping that contrary to what I've read online, the painting will be hanging inside and not in the hallway. As I enter, I realise that the 'museum' is a single tall room. My eyes take in a flush of wood: wooden floorboards, wooden cabinets and wood panelling on the walls. Wood panels around the rim of the ceiling and on them, intricate paintings of doctors in dark robes and with thick moustaches.

As I step in, I see a woman sitting by a wooden desk. Pamphlets are stacked beside her and a small tin lock box rests by her folded hands. She smiles as I walk over to pay the few euros entrance fee. As I she fills in a receipt by hand,

I ask her about Brouillet and the painting I'd been expecting to see in the hall.

'Charcot is not here but in China. At an exhibit. Actually, in recent years it has become quite popular so for a few months it is being lent to a museum there.'

I'm disappointed, but try not to let it show. I was hoping to see the painting myself, without the blur of onscreen pixels interfering. In the disappointment, a thought flashes through me. If the painting is not here, how can it shake whatever has seized me loose? A part of me, one that couldn't speak it, thought that looking at hysteria's past would help me understand myself and the seizures a little better.

The woman hurries away to a small bookshelf and returns carrying a heavy volume. She lays out a textbook with the painting printed, glossy, across two pages. A fold runs down the centre of the painting, splitting Blanche from her audience.

'If you are interested in Charcot', she says, 'there is his equipment upstairs. He was known for his work in neurology and ahh ...' she pauses to reach for the right word. 'Neuroses.'

The antique stairs are steep and as I ascend, a feeling of dizziness overwhelms me. The exhibit is on a thin landing with an ornate iron rail. There is just enough room for one person. The passage is slightly tilted so as I look into the glass displays, I feel as though I'm being sucked back onto the first floor. Being surrounded by wood makes it all the more sickly, as if I were on a ship rocking through light waves.

The first thing I see in the display is Charcot's face etched into a gold coin. It's the diameter of my index finger and his long-ridged nose shines as if he were being polished daily. It feels odd to see him as an ornament. Perhaps it's fitting, as his critics accused him of using the women he treated at the Tuesday sessions as displays for his theories.

Next, I look down and see two cylinder-like objects with smooth, flattened edges. Perhaps made of metal, they are covered in white cotton that is worn through and greyed. I think of a cotton pad, damp and grey-black after I remove my eye make-up at the end of the day. The spheres are attached, thin wires snaking, to a machine. Once I see the wires, the purpose of the machine registers. A breath catches in my chest: they are electrodes. The cylinders are flat so they can be pressed to a person's temples. The cotton is worn and grey from being held, again and again, to the skulls of patients. The howling woman sinks into my stomach as I try to translate the small white card above the machine:

Diapason électrique

M. Charcot a fait à l'Hospice de la Salpêtrière au mois d'août 1892 une curieuse leçon sur un nouveau procédé de traitement de certaines affections du système nerveux par des vibrations mécaniques.

Electric tuning fork

M. Charcot gave a curious lesson at the Hospice de
la Salpêtrière in August, 1892, on a new method of
treating certain affections of the nervous system by
mechanical vibrations.

Next to the machine is a photo. Rows of people's faces in
different positions. I see a woman with neat, dark hair and
a face that looks a bit like mine. In one photo she is blank-
faced. In the next, her right eye winces. My eyes skip ahead
to the last photo of her. The fourth panel is the worst. She is
caught between a shriek and a smile; her mouth is twisted
up on one side. Measuring it are metal clamps; it looks like
a fine pair of pliers have grasped her smile.

I feel shaken. Charcot was known for his work with
hypnotism; he thought women and men with hysteria were not 'mad' but ill. He kept them out of asylums,
except, I read later, when he wanted to discipline them.
Blanche Wittmann was kept in a cell for seven months
after a fit where she broke windows and tore her clothes
and sheets. Despite this, and the sensational nature of
the Tuesday sessions, I hadn't realised electrotherapy was
used as a treatment. Mistakenly, I'd thought despite
the time – a time where the mentally ill and poor were
locked away – that electricity was neither needed nor
administered.

Oh god, the women, I think. When I return to our
room I talk to Mum about feeling sick with it and she says,
'You can't think of it too much' but the thoughts are living
inside of me now. It feels too much to see them as me and

me as them. Our lives connected through an invisible line – a charged wire – of illness.

It was naïve to think that electricity was not part of treatment in the 18th and 19th centuries, yet the history of Charcot I have encountered has written out the electrodes. The women in the paintings shriek and writhe of their own accord, not because of the wires attached to them.

After I fall into this thought, I look for the pain in the hospital walls. I read about dermographism. Charcot experimented with inscribing on his patients' skin; at the time, the skin's ability to take on these inscriptions was believed to be evidence of 'extreme suggestibility', writes philosopher and art historian Georges Didi-Huberman. He also writes that dermographism became 'a vehicle for medical authority to exert its power'.

A doctor at the Salpêtrière – a hospital by the Seine – wrote that, 'If we lightly trace a name or a figure on the shoulders, chest, arms, or thighs of our patient, we see, almost instantly a bright red line appear. Two minutes later, the letter or the inscription appears in the form of a pale pink line.' This line could stay transcribed on the woman's body for months. In 1878, Blanche was subjected to dermographism. Her name was traced on her chest, and the name of the hospital in which she would live most of her life, 'Salpêtrière', on her stomach. She was etched, a physician's canvas. I think of how I live in fear of people learning of my mental illness. Having it drawn – almost tattooed – on me would ache.

It is easy to look at medical history and dismiss some

practices as pure cruelty but I think it is more nuanced. The doctors at the Salpêtrière wanted to help, but that does not mean that they understood their patients' experiences. Charcot wanted to document their experiences and find a way to 'cure' the women (and the few men) he treated. He *saw* them. As Freud said of him, 'He was not a reflective man, not a thinker: he had the nature of an artist – he was, as he himself said, a "visuel", a man who sees … He used to look again and again at the things he did not understand, to deepen his impression of them day by day.' The concept of 'seeing' is apparent throughout his methods, given his use of anatomical artists and photographers, as well as allowing the women to move about the hospital freely. He let the world see his patients too. But seeing is not understanding; without empathy, even with hopes of taking this illness away from Blanche and the women around her, treatments can still harm.

The women's bodies increasingly became public displays, objects to be looked at in fascination, yet some patients found a power in this. Blanche, admitted to the Salpêtrière as Marie Wittmann, was eighteen years old when she walked through those hospital gates. By then, she had seen five of her eight siblings die, as well as her mother, who died quickly and unexpectedly. Her father, an abusive man who had attempted to throw Blanche out of a window when she was a child, had been admitted to Saint-Anne, an asylum where he would live until his death. Too old to be cared for in a foster home like her younger siblings, Blanche returned at fifteen to live with a fur merchant whom she had worked for as an apprentice between the ages of twelve and four-teen. She had previously escaped him after the older man made aggressive sexual advances and attempted to harm her. But after her mother's death, Blanche was forced back to her abuser, who raped her over the next eight months until she fled again to become a hospital worker. Through-out Blanche's life, and particularly while living with the abuser, she experienced 'attacks' where she would convulse, and have tremors and episodes of 'nervousness'.

From this to her life at Salpêtrière, Blanche became a medical model in all senses. Her identity literally changed; she switched from her birth name 'Marie' to 'Blanche', as literary scholar Asti Hustvedt writes in *Medical Muses*: 'this inexplicable shift in nomenclature seems to foreshadow the transformation in her identity that would take place over the next decade at Salpêtrière'.

At first, Blanche's symptoms fell into those ordinar-ily categorised as 'hysteric'. She fit, but like all hysterics, she could not be explained. After a violent episode where Blanche tore her sheets and broke windows, Charcot locked her away in an asylum. This was a punishment; Blanche, writes Hustvedt, 'lost almost all of this freedom to move about and spent far more time confined to a cell'. Writer Jules Claretie, who spent time at Salpêtrière by invitation from Charcot wrote in his novel, *Les Amours d'un Interne*, that 'To descend one degree further into that hell where human reason has been swallowed up in a black nothing-ness! This was the greatest fear of the hysterics, who were still free to come and go.'

After seven months in the asylum, Blanche was returned to Charcot's ward, where her symptoms became increasingly prototypical, more in line with Charcot's definition of hysteria. Unlike before her incarceration in the asylum, Blanche now experienced what Charcot called 'hysterogenic zones'. When these parts of Blanche's body were pressed, she would become ill. Philosopher and visitor to the Salpêtrière Joseph Delboeuf says that with the 'hysterogenic zones', Blanche's doctors 'played her as though she were a piano … and he played any tune'. And so, as Hustvedt writes, 'Blanche was held up as living proof of the Salpêtrière School's theories, the embodiment of Charcot's symptomology.'

There is contention about the nature of Blanche's illness – questions arising of fabrication and deception. Of the Tuesday sessions, physician Axel Munthe, who worked at the Salpêtrière, says that 'these stage performances of the Salpêtrière before the public of *tout Paris* were nothing but an absurd face, a hopeless muddle of truth and cheating'. Munthe believed that it was the patients who possessed 'amazing cunning' in performing but he also criticised the medical professionals around them for hypnotism, saying that, 'many of these girls spent their days in a state of semi-trance, their brains bewildered by all sorts of absurd suggestions'.

I think that Hustvedt says it best: 'Human beings, as a rule, adapt to fit social norms, and patients adapt to medical standards'. Blanche, I think, did not knowingly alter her behaviour, and thus illness, but her body did what it must to survive. She might have become carried away at the Tuesday sessions; her 'performance' directly affected her quality of life. The most popular sessions would be taken to different hospitals; Blanche visited Hàtel Dieu Hospital. For a woman whose movements were restricted to the Salpêtrière, who had known loss and violence, I imagine that dramatising her illness before others would be worth the small luxuries she was afforded in return.

On her deathbed, Blanche said about her time with Charcot and the accusations of feigning: 'If we were put to sleep, if we had fits, it was because it was impossible for us to do otherwise. Besides, it's not as though it was pleasant!' It is understandable that the world around you will alter your experience. Blanche lived most of her life at the Salpêtrière, oscillating between life as a patient and as an employee. Being around Charcot and his patients shaped her and her illness. And because of this influence, she came to be Charcot's most famous patient. Her life was transformed; she moved from hardship to another, more forgiving existence.

But after Charcot's death in 1893, his school ceased to exist. Neurology did not need Blanche any more. She stayed at the Salpêtrière, though, where she worked as a technician at the laboratory established by radiologist Dr Charles Infroit. It was the beginning of the twentieth century and the dangers of radiology were not yet understood. Blanche, like Infroit after her, developed cancer from her proximity to radiation. To slow its progression, her fingers were removed one by one as, eventually, were her left hand, forearm and remaining arm. Her legs, too, were amputated. Blanche died in 1913 at fifty-four years of age, leaving behind only the photographs, drawings and paintings of her time as the Queen of Hysterics.

But when I'm at the Musée d'Histoire de la Médecine, staring at electrical equipment and wincing at a fading green label that reads 'Batterie Médicale Superieure: Grande Capacité', I don't yet know of Blanche's legacy. I know only of Charcot. His life is the one that's written about, even venerated as a great medical gift, and so it is him I had thought of. Now, I see the women pictured before me. Women who lived at the perimeter of discussions on psychosomatic symptoms.

I look at a small sketch in light pencil of a woman's body – it is not clear whether this is a woman from the Salpêtrière. I do not recognise it as either Blanche nor Augustine, Charcot's best-known patients. The lines are crude and there is no shading, but I see her clearly. Her mouth is in the shape of an 'O' and the folds of her naked body ripple over themselves. Behind the glass, a small cardboard tag says:

Croquis de Paul Richer

La grande attaque hystérique est toujours annoncée par des prodromes (signes préscurseurs). Elle se décompose ensuite en quatre phases: la période épileptoïde, la période des grands mouvements, la période des attitudes passionnelles, la période de délire.

Sketch of Paul Richer

The great hysterical attack is always heralded by
warning signs (precursor signs). It is broken then into
four phases: the epileptoid period, the period of great
movements, the period of passionate attitudes, the
period of delirium.

I see her, my fingers pressed up against the glass as if I could
push against it and move closer. As if it were plastic wrap,
not locked glass. I feel faint looking at the pain shaping its
way through her. The lack of detail in her face makes her
every hysterical woman. She shrieks for all of us.

I walk back downstairs, hand firmly gripping the rail
as if I were mirroring the contortions of Blanche's fingers
in Brouillet's painting. At the base of the stairs, the bannis-
ter ends in a pole around which a snake wraps itself. An orb
sits on top with the snake's split tongue arching over the
globe. I recognise it as the Rod of Asclepius; Asclepius the
son of Apollo and Greek god of medicine. It's a reminder
that the pattern of becoming ill then trying to heal is an
ancient one.

By the end of the staircase are two displays: a
wooden anatomical figure and a small, ornate table with
an embalmed human foot in its centre, centred by four
embalmed ears, now grey. Coloured tiles and the mosaic
surrounding the foot mean that unless you look closely,
the ears are easy to miss. The anatomical figure has been
carved with a strong jaw and calm, closed eyes and I

imagine him watching over me as well as the odd assembly of visitors who have passed through since the museum opened in 1954.

I walk over to the woman with her small tin moneybox and ask her to translate a sign I had seen by the entrance. She is kind, and even seems excited about engaging with a visitor. She follows me to a large wooden table with a glass wheel fixed into it that is almost as tall as I am. It spins when pushed, rubbing against leather-padded cushions. Creating friction, I guess correctly. The woman nods: a patient would hold a wire connected to the wheel as it spins, giving a slight shock. She reads the sign out in snippets, her long pauses allowing the movement of the contraption to embed itself in my mind:

Machine du type de RAMSDEN construite par DUMOTIEZ, XIXe siècle.

L'électricité statique était recommandee pour le traitement des maladies nerveuses, les neuralgies et les affections rhumatismates.

RAMSDEN-type machine built by DUMOTIEZ, in the 19th century.

Static electricity was recommended for the treatment of nervous illnesses, neuralgias and rheumatic diseases.

The woman then turns to me, her eyes on mine. 'The rich', she explains, 'would often have literary salons and began to have salons where they administered electricity, too. They would watch a person hold on to the wire as the wheel spun.' I am nodding as she speaks, imagining a scene like Brouillet's painting but with fully dressed women. They had more control over their experience with electricity. The woman continues, 'They thought it would cure maladies like skin diseases as well as, uh, nervous disorders.' I listen carefully, beginning to realise that she might feel awkward discussing mental illness with a young woman she does not know.

The machine is from the nineteenth century, but earlier than Charcot. Yet to my eye, the only difference between this and Charcot's contraption is its size. The machine before me looks more like a small, hand-built stage at a community centre; with the introduction of central electricity, Charcot could take his machines from room to room. In theory, the six thousand patients at the Salpêtrière could easily access electrotherapy as a treatment whether they experienced hysteria or not.

As the afternoon stretches on, I realise that being in the space of the museum – a place tinged by history running through it like a current – brings a tightness to my throat. I have always distanced myself from the history of madness. The treatments and women locked away. It was easier to forget the history of mental health treatments than to see myself as sharing in the modern incarnation of that legacy. I've been preoccupied with the failings of today's psych wards and didn't want to face the women who suffered centuries before me.

There's a photo series by Gordon (Don) Charles Montgomery, who used to work as a boiler-man in Prestwich Hospital, showing patients who lived in the psychiatric ward throughout the late 1970s to early 90s. One image in particular catches me. A woman in her seventies lies in the sun, her pink floral dress riding up to her thighs. She looks so peaceful and girlish lying there. Her wrinkles settle gently in the sunlight. It's as though she's forgotten her age, away from the world. She is enjoying the sunshine. I think of her as happy, although the serenity of her face causes her wrinkles to slant down in the shape of a frown. This photo of her in the sun has been the most I can bear to think of an age (one that, in some places, is ongoing) where mental illness was 'cured' with locked doors.

The day before I visited the Musée d'Histoire de la Médecine, I had tried on an expensive bag and a $2000 leather jacket at Galeries Lafayette. They cost more than the bond to my small house but I pulled them onto me, pretending that I belonged. It was as if I was trying on another skin. A life where bags and coats like these were possible and the trials of medication and therapy were not my life. But looking at these people in the museum – Blanche being painted as she seized, the body of Augustine arching up as if she were being exorcised – I feel as if I understand.

I'm not sure I fit here (if anywhere) but I see them fully, if not in the walls of this museum, then in my mind.

And through the way they lived their lives, I am beginning to feel seen by them.

*

It has been fourteen days since I have had a seizure. I think they have disintegrated. A sense of falling apart is the best way to describe what has happened. The seizures were once bulking, heavy things that would grab me, unrelenting as I fell through the pattern of it all. It came to be a dance with designed steps.

Zoom in eyes, a stranger's hands, stretching walls, flickering lights.

One, two-three. One, two-three.

Now, the monster has become dust. Tiny particles, grey and soft, that lay themselves over me. I breathe them in and the atoms of them join the atoms of me. We mix, like milk that clouds for a moment before settling in the deep brown of my coffee. Dust-me means that the seizures don't come heavy but I live – unanchored – with sprinklings of unreality.

I still take in the eyes and mouths of people greedily. The shapes of them so different. As though I have only seen half a dozen faces before, they are all fresh. It takes a while but I realise that I've begun to think fiction is real – a strange swap from believing myself to be unrecognisable or worse, dead. I know intellectually that Anna Karenina is not walking around nor Clarissa Dalloway living in a cosy unaffordable home in London. But I don't feel this to be true. If I'm being honest, most days they feel as alive as I do. In a way, I've felt this before, when I first fell in love with reading. I came to reading later than most and so my late teens were spent catching up and falling into written lives. But then, while I imagined myself on the page too, my perception of myself wasn't murky. My new sense of distrust that a novel doesn't remain in my hands but is living in a world more real than my own has a dark undertone; reality is crumblier than it ever was before.

Yet unlike the seizures, the dust doesn't scare me. It's more an embrace – a new take on an old world. When I finish reading a great book, I see the world a little differently. The dust feels like an extension of great writing, not the name of something in the DSM.

I don't want to go back to therapy. Perhaps I'm in the honeymoon phase of unreality. Am I hysterical? I feel calm and safe. This touch of unreality is almost cosy compared to living through the seizures, where I was scared to live in my own skin. I return to thinking of the seizures – or now, this hazy unreality – as my masked protector.

*

I go to the Salpêtrière. For answers, maybe. To say I was there, where women seized and fainted in a room full of curious men. I walk past a grimy train station, under a thick bridge with tents and couches lining a fence, to find it. It's an old building; it looks more like a monument than a working hospital, with its arches and ballooning oval roofs. At its centre there is a clock tower, rising three levels above the rest of the hospital. Time moves steadily, only stopping and starting for the patients dying and being born inside the hospital's wings. This was where it all began, I think, not with me but other bodies. Other women who seized up in their surroundings and lived out their lives in the Salpêtrière, being studied.

As I enter the hospital – through the arch, past the café and on to the grounds – I see a chapel to the left. It's more imposing than any church I have seen at home, let alone a hospital chapel, which is often just a room from where you can still hear the beeping of nearby machines. I follow the shape of the building, hoping to find its entrance. It is dotted with white circulation grates marked with holes in the shape of a thick cross. As I reach the door, I realise my high school French is not good enough to understand the service schedule. I am unsure whether to enter, whether the church is open. The door is heavy wood and as I press on it, it is slow to give and opens with a moan.

I take my first steps into the chapel. The floors and walls are made from the same grey limestone that you see throughout Europe. Each surface radiates cool while I try to quieten the clack of my boots as I step into the church. I can hear a service in the next room; a voice sings out, deep in chanting. I am taken to the Greek Orthodox church of my childhood and the way the priest would sing in Greek as he spread incense throughout the room. Unable to understand him, I would take to silently counting to the highest number imaginable. I usually fumbled at around

300 and would start again, exasperated, still listening to the stretch of his voice expanding throughout the church. I leave quickly and quietly, not wanting to bring attention to myself and disturb the service. I spot another woman, dressed in all black with red boots, doing the same.

Next to the chapel, I find a park. It's simple: a large rectangle dotted with trees and benches. It is beautiful but has an air of gloom on this crisp Paris day. On the edge of the park, close to the chapel's door, are people squatting. Their knees are spread, breasts arch out in points and they lift wooden slabs of varying weights above their heads. Their muscles are thick, legs and arms stocky, and they are completely still in their crouching positions. It takes a moment to register that they are rooted to the ground. The women have been carved from trees planted in the park long ago; they are forever lifting, struggling to carry their burdens.

As I walk, I see the park's name in white letters on an ornate iron-framed sign. At the top of the sign is a thick black crown surrounded by curved peaks of iron. The sign reads:

Promenade de la Hauteur

Respectez ce lieu tenu secret, véritable havre de paix qui se cache au coeur de la Salpêtrière. Ecoutez la nature, vous serez su ris!

Walk Exultantly

> Respect this place which is kept secret, a true
> haven of peace which hides itself in the heart of the
> Salpêtrière. Listen to nature, you will be known to
> laugh!

I try to listen to nature, as the sign instructs, as I walk through the Promenade de la Hauteur. I try also, as it feels I always am, to feel safe and well. As I continue to walk to the park's centre, thinking of how odd it is to try to evoke peace and safety at a hospital, I see bronzed figures. Walking towards them, I see that they too show illness. A bronze man, folded over himself, head resting on his knees. A head faces the sky open-mouthed, with resting, folded eyes. A fist, as wide as my shoulders, clenches hard. If bronze could draw blood, I imagine this fist would. I'm drawn in by these representations of illness. Illness isn't the right word – it's seeing *patients* that captures me. Reading about hysteria, I am used to the medical, the tools used on the unwell. Like at the museum, I feel as though I'm not used to seeing the patients who live with the illnesses. I am far more familiar with the worlds of those who diagnose it.

It makes sense, I tell myself, as I live in a world where the voices doing the diagnosing are the loudest. Everything I've read has been filtered through the voice of a medical professional. Except for Edith, who possessed this privilege, the depictions of women I've imagined myself beside are built on others' perceptions of them. This book, too, continues to build upon histories that might not have even been accurate when they were written. How much can I belong to them – and they me – when I possess the privilege of a voice that is heard? Even when I'm dismissed in today's medical world, I have people around me who will advocate for my health. Most importantly, I have my own spaces where I am heard. Writing my life down as I became unwell helped; I could not speak this illness aloud but could write it. I don't know what it's like to be ill and not have a voice. Mary, Katharina, Blanche spoke in ways that meant they were ostracised. To be punished for being ill, when this illness is already so punishing, is a hardship that I can never fully fathom.

In an alcove at the hospital itself were two sculptures facing each other. Separated by rows of flowers placed by mourners, the marble sculptures show two sides of the medical profession. On the left is a man in flowing robes with tightly curled hair, a handkerchief around his neck. His posture is stiff and straight, hands gently folded in his lap. He is a typical gentleman, I imagine, from the time the statue was created. Facing him, a woman is sitting slumped back. She is draped in a light dress that falls off her shoulders as her mouth drops open. Leaning on her is a crouching man and small child, each almost undressed as their heads tilt back in sickness.

It's a classic representation of illness that perseveres to this day: one of a controlled doctor faced by the uncontrolled sick. Sickness is a problem to be solved; it is the sick's lack of control that creates fear. The family is not just ill – so ill they are collapsing upon one another as their pain swells – they are in disarray. The mother is the only one clothed and even then, her feet remain bare. Illness begets poverty and vice versa. Although they are made of marble, when I look at the huddled family, my instinct is not to help them but to escape them. It's thought that the sick – whether they are experiencing physical pain, mental pain or both – should be met with the control of a professional, so they too can return to society with rational control. Essayist Marlene Benjamin writes in 'The Disordered Self', where she discusses the neuroscience, philosophy and her own lived experience of mental illness:

> Mental illness, as stigmatized, signals to most people the farthest we can go from our humanness, from what makes us human rather than mere animals, for it signals our un-reason, which sets us apart from *normal* people who are 'made in the image of God' with reason as the central signifying human feature. It is *the disorder* of the human condition. Mental illness strikes most people as marking the sufferer as closer to our animality, and thus closer to the mortality of being human.

'Most people' are repelled by illness. Then there is another set of people: those who are repelled yet fascinated, drawn in by the swoop of Blanche's frame or the twisting of Augustine's spine. I've touched this perspective, being drawn to illness through my own experience of it like a magnet being pulled forward to find its other half.

As I continue to walk through the grounds of Paris's

largest hospital, the same words echo in my mind again and again. I think, as cool air whips my face, *it is just a building*. I had hoped that being here would connect me to something more. If I hadn't felt a change at the Musée d'Histoire de la Médecine, perhaps I'd hoped I could settle for finding a place where I can be at ease in my experience. Perhaps I would not feel ill here; my experience of illness would be the norm. But a building cannot answer the knots of wires and pathways that plague my brain. No one has found a sense of peace, an ease with being hysterical, at the Salpêtrière. I do not fit here and neither did Blanche.

Marlene Benjamin writes of a fellow patient going through an outpatient program with her, a bipolar man on lithium. Benjamin recounts that, 'When it was his turn to speak I nearly wept with sorrow for him.' Before being in the outpatient program, before his illness had made the everyday difficult, he had worked as a doctor. He held a PhD and spent his life helping the sick. He said, near tears, 'now I have to find a new way of being myself, because my illness makes it impossible for me to be myself in the old way, and I don't know how to do this, or where to begin'.

I relate to him in more ways than I can write. I don't know how to exist either. I have become someone else. I cannot work the way I used to and I plan my days meticulously, spreading social events carefully throughout the week so as not to throw myself into a seizure. My life has changed; it has stilled. Yet while it is less busy, it is not more peaceful. Sitting alone, trying to read or watching the flick of my sleeping dog's tail, I think of what I've 'allowed' to happen. I think of what it means to become so over-whelmed by the world that you have to remove yourself from it. I wonder if I'll ever be able to re-enter it, not after-noons at a time but fully.

As I walk back to Le Marais from the Salpêtrière, past the arches and clipped rose bushes lining the hospital, I think of what life will be when I'm home. Paris didn't have the answers I'd hoped for. I'd expected a messiness, to be hit by the force of my experience so I could emerge out of the ashes of illness as myself again. But the day moves on and I'm grappling with the experience. A building could not offer me answers. It felt like the last hope, having exhausted professionals throughout Adelaide. I enter Boulevard de l'Hôpital and hear the chatter and laughs of nursing students. I think of what is left.

No buildings. No museums. There's only me.

V.
KATERINA

Animals get diseases, but only man falls radically into sickness.

– *Oliver Sacks*, The Man Who Mistook His Wife For a Hat

Ideas come to us as the successors to griefs, and griefs, at the moment when they change into ideas, lose some part of their power to injure the heart.

– *Marcel Proust*, In Search of Lost Time

I read Lee Kofman's *Imperfect* and am struck by a passage that so encapsulates the past year of my life. She writes:

They say most of us fluctuate between acceptance and grief, ebbing and flowing in a kind of oceanic pattern, depending on what else is going on in our lives. This view resonates with me and I came to think of bodily self-acceptance more as a verb than a noun, a verb of ongoing negotiation.

Kofman is writing about her own sense of self-acceptance in relation to the scars left by multiple surgeries, but I think this idea captures what it is like living with severe mental illness too. Not only do symptoms themselves ebb and flow, but so does my ability to accept them as a part of my daily existence. Some days are harder than others and it takes an enormous effort to shift from thinking of what I've lost to what I've gained.

The language we use around illness comes from a perspective of loss. I *fall* ill. *Suffer* from mental illness. And these are the inoffensive terms. *Crazy* and *hysterical* and *mad* are all within the everyday realm. I am guilty of using these words too, not being any better than the world I have been born into. But I try to make a shift. I have grown from my experience of mental illness. I did not wish to grow in such a way – to understand the complex systems of medicalisation and the hoops one must jump through (and pay for) to be seen by a psychiatrist – but I have. My life has also grown simpler. I limit my day within the confines of what my body can handle. While it means some days I am particularly isolated, I also enjoy the comfort of watching sunshine pour through my window while my dog stretches and groans happily beside me.

I have also grown into a more complete love. My partner has not retreated from this shifting illness but endeavoured to understand it. At the same time, he hasn't made me feel more incapacitated than I am. I had no idea at the beginning that was exactly what I would need, but it came to me as I spoke to the psychologist I was eventually referred to. When my hallucinations reach a certain intensity, I instinctively blink as if that action will wash away the frightening imagery my mind imposes. Mathew, seeing this as I stand paralysed in the living room, comes up to me and says, 'What's up, Blinky Bill?' while throwing an arm around my shoulders. His humour breaks the moment of fear and, now, I am able to grin back at him. Recounting this in therapy, I feel my eyes brimming with tears and am overwhelmed with gratitude. My psychologist smiles back at me, happy for me. A partnership like this is a privilege.

My parents, also living through their own grief at the challenges I face, have given me their support. Mum dropping dinner off at my home after a long work week; Dad cheerfully telling me about a new recipe for homemade dog food he's trying for both his dog and mine, before tentatively asking, 'How is your health?' These acts of care have upheld a sense of normalcy throughout a rough few years of learning to understand my own shifting mind and body. I am grateful that we have worked to build relationships where we can communicate our needs with one another, rushing in to share the weight that illness unexpectedly dumps upon you. But some part of me knows that it is luck that I have these people in my life who are willing to try to understand my complex illness. I have won a lottery to have parents who, while flawed like anyone else, are present and care deeply about my ability to move through the world. I am lucky where so many women are not.

And somehow, mixed with deep appreciation for my family, on the best days I have come to feel love towards myself. Reading back parts of this book, I learn I am resilient. I learn that, when necessary, I'm a good actor. Yes, people will care for me when I'm ill but I'm capable of caring for myself even at my sickest. If I was alone in this, I would struggle but I would survive.

It would be easier – and perhaps more natural with a brain like mine that is prone to travelling down the anxiety track – to think of loss. I could count the friend who, after I mentioned going to a psychiatrist, looked at me fearfully over our lattes. She hasn't contacted me since, and in quiet moments I find myself still grieving that loss. I could talk about the what-ifs. What if, when this book meets the world, I can no longer find employment? What if I lose more friends or even family? But I'm learning I can't think of those eventualities; not when writing has kept me afloat. Not when I possess both the privilege of being able to speak and being supported in voicing the shape of my own mental illness. As Hélène Cixous writes, 'It is this hunger for flesh and for tears, our appetite for living, that, at the tip of forsaken fingers, makes a pencil grow.' In the time I've been absent from the world, weakened by illness but craving life, my pencil grew and granted me the strength to write, and by doing so, try to accept my illness.

*

I fell ill a few months before my twenty-fourth birthday. The nature of the illness meant that it took me a little while to realise. I didn't know I was sick because my sense of permanence and earthliness was faltering. When you feel inhuman, your mind doesn't necessarily register that you need to see a doctor. It feels deep and sinister, but also natural in a way.

Years after first becoming ill, I read the work of violinist and writer Jessica Chiccehitto Hindman, who in her memoir *Sounds Like Titanic* writes about the experience of fear during her panic attacks, and something clicks. She falls ill at a similar time in her life to me and writes: 'For the early twenties, a particularly cruel age to be struck down by fear, is a stage in life when tremendous bravery is required of a woman – the bravery to discover what she wants, what she cannot abide, what she needs to make a living and be among the living.' Reading her words, for the first time I feel a sympathy, not for myself in this moment as a person living in a sick body, but for a past self. One who, while used to mental illness, was not used to this intensity. This feeling of everything coming undone. One who didn't realise how young and sick they were. One who didn't know how much bravery they'd need in the coming years.

I was young and sick and striving for this idea of a cure and so it took a year to come to therapy. I move my body into the waiting room with a sickly pothos plant and the same embroidered chair I find myself sitting in every time. I'd been in other waiting rooms: those of hospitals, GPs and psychiatrists' offices. I'd been turned down from others, once via a one-line text message. But it was in this office that I was given some relief. It was not what I had hoped for (a cure), nor what I had expected either (nothing).

In my head, I call my psych Dr Robert. It's a Beatles reference from side two of *Revolver* that Mathew first came up with and I think it has lingered for the irony. Dr Robert is a psychologist; he does *not* prescribe drugs, over the counter or otherwise. Mathew and I laugh about it until we forget the joke and it just becomes my psych's name. In these ways, I manage to hold on to myself. It's no easy task to do so through the process of building enough trust with someone to reveal how ill I am, scratching away the mask of make-up and jokes and thick books I carry with me into the waiting room.

Later I will read Jessica Friedmann's *Things That Helped* and think of how Friedmann writes of her relationship with a therapist, Kristy. Because she 'can't help [herself]' she criticises the painting in Kristy's office: 'I think it is terrible; Kristy tells me again, calmly, that she enjoys looking at it. I admire her for the way she puts me in my place without making me feel small.' This stays with me; I admire Dr Robert for how he both laughs at my jokes and takes me seriously.

Every time I have seen Dr Robert, he is wearing a three-piece suit. Even in the dry Adelaide summer, a silk handkerchief peeks out of his jacket pocket, which makes me smile. He looks distinctly European, but he speaks with an Australian accent. Sometimes I wonder if the illusion of European professionalism would be broken if I were to see him outside of his office, perhaps in track pants or shorts. Try as I might, I cannot conjure the image. He lives forever in that space, suited and listening.

At the first session with Dr Robert, I tell him about the seizures and he replies that he thought it was a 'normal day' of diagnosis. I explain that my GP wrote 'anxiety' (*technically* true because, this, I also have) on the mental healthcare plan because she was afraid that if she wrote 'psychogenic non-epileptic seizures', my claim would be denied. He nods as I speak and goes on to explain that he has never had a patient experiencing psychosomatic seizures. He is honest. He tells me he will do some research before we next see each other. He also says he is unsure if the symptoms will ever go away, but he hopes to help me improve my quality of life. At the time, I am wary of anyone who believes they could heal me. I've learnt that often means they aren't listening. This admission from him means I allow myself to trust just a little.

*

I watch an episode of the ABC show *You Can't Ask That* and nod at the people with schizophrenia describing their hallucinations. I understand, in a way. I see balls of coloured light and checkered lines and lights flicker violently when I have a seizure. Mathew asks me to turn it off. 'Why?' I ask. He replies, 'It's too sad'. I say, 'They're me' but the words don't quite form in my mouth. I'm them and they're me and I wonder if maybe my story is not for everyone. Maybe it's for the people who've thought, 'I might be mad', and had people look at them funny in the street. Maybe it's our story and though we try and share it in our own ways, people might never understand. Those who live in Susan Sontag's 'kingdom of the well' may not be able to touch our stories.

*

Dr Robert buys a book on treatment options for my condition – *Psychogenic Non-Epileptic Seizures: A Guide* by Lorna Myers – and in our fifth appointment, lends it to me. Inside, there is a cartoon cat with scraggly black fur arched up and shrieking at a carefree terrier:

> Figure 5: A non-threatening puppy is interpreted as
> dangerous by this anxious cat.

It takes a cartoon for me to realise how tiring it is to be constantly compared to others: people with epilepsy, the 'mad' and, especially, 'anxious' cats. I start taking mental notes, criticisms of the book. Not for myself, I think, but to protect the *other* patients. It takes me a day or two to realise that there are no other patients. It's just me.

*

I read an interview with young adult novelist John Green and see myself in him. Interviews can have this benefit for writers and readers alike: to make us see what we have in common, whether we're famous or unknown. It's not writing that connects us, but illness. Green's earliest memories include OCD, like mine. He tells journalist Alexandra Alter that, 'I spent a lot of my childhood consumed with obsessive worry and dread', and so he wrote *Turtles All the Way Down* to 'help people who struggle with that terror to feel less alone'. He wrote not only for others, but also himself after a particularly difficult period of illness: 'it was difficult to write about anything else. The topic demanded itself.' Like Green, I want someone to read my work and to feel that they are not alone in their hallucinations or episodes of mental illness. That mental illness is not something you invite, and it can be lived through. This is what I hope but it is not why I wrote this book. My illness, too, demanded to be written. At first, I thought I wrote to heal myself of the seizures. Now, I'm not so sure. I think, now that it's on the page, *Hysteria* healed me of the idea that I could not live with the seizures. It healed me of my fear of being sick forever.

*

Dr Robert lets my sessions run late. They bleed into the next hour. One day, I stay for two and a half. When I leave, my mouth is dry and my jaw aching from so much introspection. I wonder if he lets my sessions run over because I need it, or because I'm interesting to him. I'm his first patient with PNES. Maybe it's both. Or perhaps I'm overthinking it. What if it's just that his afternoon is free and he's feeling generous? I might not be as special as I think I am.

I start to wonder what will happen when the sessions

end; I count down the ten government rebate sessions with a sense of foreboding. One week, I lose track of which session I'm up to and find I'm too scared to ask, too scared to learn that my time is up. I cannot afford to come back without the rebate, even if these sessions are the only thing keeping me in touch with the possibility of a well self. Without a rebate, they cost more than a week's rent. On the tenth session, Dr Robert recommends I extend for another four. I have to go back to my GP, but I'm grateful to be given this extra time. It's medically recommended and so, to me, feels legitimate. I don't stop to wonder if what I feel I need holds any legitimacy. Instead, the damaged part of me feels special, as if being this sick is a competition and I have come out a winner with my fourteen sessions. I imagine Susan Sontag being disappointed in me – her clever eyes boring into me from the cover of *Illness as Metaphor*. I make a note in my phone to bring this up with Dr Robert in our next session.

*

Some days I am still angry. Angry that this has happened at all, that it's still happening. That the rest of the world continues to live in health. Of course, when I am angry I cannot imagine that anyone else is suffering. It is me, alone, who hurts. Waiting for a bus, I'll see someone walk by, chatting with a friend. Perhaps they'll laugh and my jaw will set. Sometimes it's that I notice there are no dark rings under their eyes. *How dare they sleep at night*. They don't massage their jaws, trying to ease the joints that have locked up in the night after seeing a movie that tactlessly portrayed suicide. *How easy it must be to be them.*

I hold on to my anger for weeks until I realise that maybe these people are looking back at me. Maybe they see someone in a well-cut jacket, one on which I spent my first big writing payday. If I took a long walk with my dog that day, perhaps I'm smiling and they don't see the rage and the illness. Maybe they look at the bright lipstick or the hair I dye in increasingly outrageous colours. They don't see hallucinations and fear. They see someone like themselves, or maybe even someone they wish to be. I console myself with this thought and feel the anger slipping.

*

One night, I watch *House on Haunted Hill* (1959). A millionaire, played by the wonderfully spooky Vincent Price, offers $10 000 to five people who agree to spend the night locked in a haunted house with him and his wife. Among the guests is Dr David Trent (Alan Marshal), a psychiatrist who specialises in hysteria, and when I hear this, the sense that this movie is separate from my everyday is shattered. I hadn't expected to find this view of hysteria lingering so late in popular culture, so close to the 60s. I almost don't continue but then a character discovers a severed head in her suitcase and I'm drawn back in by the gaudy screams. Shaken, she approaches the rest of the group but when they go to see what has distressed her, the head has disappeared. Dr Trent says to her, 'Nora, I think you're a little upset. Would you care for a sedative?' and I begin to shake too, consumed with laughter. I'm not sure what it means to relate to a woman who sees what others cannot, who braves something hidden from those around her and is offered sedatives in response. But the tension that had accumulated in me since I heard the word 'hysteria' dispels. I wonder if it's because this word, which is not spoken but underlines my interactions with the medical world – and in some ways, my existence – has been taken and dropped into a campy horror movie. It's ridiculous, but so is all of it. In the film, a skeleton is listed in the credits as played 'by himself'. I love it. I think it is a distinctly human experience to feel we have found the perfect book, film, album to encapsulate how we feel at that very moment. How strange that *House on Haunted Hill* winks at me, beckoning me to believe that it is not me who is mad but the medicalised world around me.

*

I've come to think that illness can inspire feelings of both guilt and specialness. Susan Sontag in *Illness as Metaphor* writes that, 'the romantic treatment of death asserts that people were made singular, made more interesting, by their illnesses'. And if your illness resists definition? If you are left living as a question mark? How does this affect your ability to see yourself as you are, not as someone made unique by an illness nor marred by ruminating on 'Did

I do this to myself?' Later in the essay, Sontag writes on mental illness:

> In the twentieth century the cluster of metaphors and attitudes formerly attached to TB split up and are parcelled out ... Some features of TB go to insanity: the notion of the sufferer as a hectic, reckless creature of passionate extremes, someone too sensitive to bear the horrors of the vulgar, everyday world.

How can I resist the metaphors that have spent years being solidified in our cultural imagining when there is no alternative presented to me? Sometimes I wonder if I am so mad that I cannot tell I am making this up – that I truly am that 'reckless creature' Sontag speaks of.

In the end, it's Dr Robert who tells me I shouldn't blame myself for my illness. Or rather, it's Dr Robert to whom I listen when he tells me this. He reminds me I didn't want to be sick. We practise this conversation again and again. Each time I get a little better. I'm still trying to learn it's not my fault but after months upon months, I'm moving away from blame. I wonder whether my ability to believe Dr Robert when he says these words, but not myself, comes from the part of my mind that made me sick. If I can no longer trust my sense of reality on some days, how can I trust myself?

*

When we talk about illness, the term 'cost' often means an emotional one; a toll on the body, perhaps even the mind. At least, I think this is true in Australia, where we have a publicly funded universal healthcare system. But for me the process of becoming ill and then trying to find a way back to health was a financially expensive one.

I cannot bear to count it precisely so I will say I have spent (or perhaps my mind has 'cost') between $1000 and $2000 at the psychiatrist. Four hundred a session, $100 or so back on rebate. Perhaps two months' worth of visits. My parents paid for the psychiatrist until they could no longer afford it. I am privileged and thankful they were able to provide anything at all.

I have not been back to the psychiatrist since starting to see Dr Robert; I have told him I cannot afford to, and so I juggle between my GP and him. Even so, I couldn't afford to see Dr Robert without the government rebate, and within this, if he had not personally reduced his gap. The sessions become possible for me after this alteration – on my income, the difference is prohibitive. Too unwell to work as I once had, at this time I had reduced my shifts so they just covered my rent and food, with a little left over for medical expenses. Looking back, I think I probably wasn't well enough to work. But that is the privilege of looking back.

It is only now, a little more well and with a little more clarity, that I think about how the CT scan and EEG were bulk-billed. In my experience, when the problem is with my brain, as opposed to my mind, it is much cheaper.

My parents and I would still have that money if the problem were just a little different. Yet even within this, I am privileged. My challenges would be dramatically more difficult if I lived in a country without a universal healthcare system, or if I lived in a regional or remote area of Australia where medical services are much harder to reach. Or if I made a little less money or knew less about how the medical industry works. It takes months for me to become well enough to realise this, and once I do, it is once again hard to resist the sweeping feel of anger.

*

One night at home I start seeing little coloured shapes moving. They flash neon-orange, purple, blue, electric-green. I'm brushing my teeth and feel a tightness start in my chest. I watch the shapes – they look almost like tadpoles – dot across the white walls of my bathroom. I look to the floor, hoping the splotch of the brown tiles will break up the vision but the tadpoles continue to dance across my eyes.

In moments like these, sometimes fear falls away. I am so transfixed by the unearthly quality of what I'm seeing. I once told a friend that it can be nice; if someone is in the middle of a long speech while the hallucinations unfold, it can be a sweet respite. This is true some of the time (and it makes for a better explanation, as it doesn't scare away new friends). Other times, it's deeply frightening to have your sense of reality stripped away in the most mundane of moments.

The neon tadpoles continue and I walk to the bedroom, hugging my arms around myself in the worn *Star Wars* t-shirt I sleep in. I find my way to Mathew and shuffle next to him. He is reading: a thick science fiction book he bought secondhand. I imagine I can smell the yellowed pages.

'Hallucinations. Distract. Me?'

My words are leaving me slowly as they always do, as though the ability to see what is not there severs the part of my brain connected to language from my throat.

Mathew puts his arm around me; my shoulders push in and I feel small in the nicest way. The panic is still circling in my throat and I try to keep my breathing steady, practising focusing on my breath as I've learnt in meditation. I try, but I can't tell if it's working. Mathew takes out his phone and opens a game app. My head leans on his shoulder as we unscramble words. I try to concentrate on the letters. My mind is slow; my shallow breaths have left me light-headed but I keep looking at the letters.

'Wistful,' I almost-wheeze and Mathew types it in.

After a few minutes, the hallucinations fade but I'm still left reeling around panic. I feel air catch in the back of my throat. I know I'm close to the whistle of the panic attack setting in and from there, it is even harder to disperse. I think of the time I was walking Suzie alone and my heart sped in my chest, my legs too weak to hold me upright. I'd had to lean against fences, pulling my body home between frequent stops. It had taken me thirty minutes to walk half a block. Once home, I slept for hours.

I push my mind back to the letters.

'Lift.'

My vision begins to blur and I realise I've been staring at the phone so intently that I haven't blinked. I look down to my hands and realise they're balled up into tightly woven fists. I stretch out my fingers and allow a slow breath out. It feels like a heatwave breaking, a cool breeze spreading its way through my body.

Hours later, I will lie in bed unable to sleep and wonder if what I've seen is not a hallucination at all. What if it's a 'floater', that vague term I've heard mentioned but never paid attention to? I open my phone, the blue glow lighting up the bedroom in eerie hues. I don't allow myself to think it as I type but I sense the thought at the edge of my body: *What if all this time you've been well? What if you're just a little dramatic?*

I decide that allaboutvision.com is a reputable enough source at 1 am and I learn that floaters are small specks or cobwebs, often grey. They are nothing like my experience and the relief born from this knowledge dislodges the fist that has been hovering in my chest. I turn off the blue-lit screen and lie awake in the darkness. I feel the weight of my dog's head resting on my feet. Mathew breathes heavily beside me, sleeping calmly. I close my eyes and find myself drifting off to a phrase methodically running through my head, as if I were counting sheep, or I am a child again and I have convinced Yiayia to read me a story.

I haven't made this up.

*

In an essay for *Meanjin* called 'This Woman Is Hysterical', Fiona Wright discusses her own illness, rumination syndrome, which she says 'exists, officially, in two different spheres, or in both simultaneously, or even somewhere somehow nebulous and in-between'. As does mine, Wright's illness exists both within the DSM and the ICD (the *International Statistical Classification of Diseases and Related Health Problems*). I know what it's like to have a nebulous illness, having been tossed from psychiatry to neurology and back.

And so, at first, I held on fiercely to the 'Psychogenic Non-Epileptic Seizures' diagnosis. I could say it quickly, roll this odd term out of my mouth as if it were something to be ashamed of. The name, although it means little, gave my illness some solidity. But over months of settling into this sickness – the everyday washing over its ambiguities and strangeness – I've shed that diagnosis.

Wright continues in her astounding essay, writing:

> There's a part of me that wishes it were still called
> hysteria, because at least the gendered and cultural
> assumptions that underpin that word are transparent,
> in a way the newer words are not.

Everyone who I've spoken to knows what 'hysteria' means when I mention that my illness would have once been called by this name. Yet 'PNES' is so unknown that even a woman I met who shared my condition had not heard this term. She went by 'functional neurological disorder' (I played with this wording later, too). I realise, at times, I've used this ambiguous language to hide behind. Stigma is a tricky thing and as Dr Robert has told me, you can never tell who it will emerge from. But now that I'm a little more settled in my diagnosis – a little bolder – I go by the somewhat vague but technically correct 'mental illness'.

And at times, I share Wright's opinion too. If it were still called 'hysteria', maybe the medical profession would feel less secure in assigning a person to the 'unknown' category and forwarding them on to the next specialist. Perhaps it would mean that the literature would pause before aligning this illness with accusations of malingering. But then again, perhaps not.

Sometimes it feels counterproductive talking about labels but I think when health feels so far away, the smallest steps towards dignity in treatment are life-changing. When you know that you will be floating through the healthcare system – making mental healthcare plans, buying antidepressants, budgeting for therapy – for most of your life, that vague hope of progress in how you are treated makes all the difference. If in fifteen years I am still listening to a GP tell me not to be ashamed when I have merely sat down and asked for a medication refill, I am not sure how I will bear it. Even worse is imagining a young woman staggering through the same questions I have and still having few answers to live with. Worse than living in limbo – coming to terms with the absence of a 'cure', just management – is living in a medical world that doesn't wish to accept nor understand what is happening.

Maybe this is all to say that I hope we can move to a place of better understanding. Oliver Sacks discusses case histories in *The Man Who Mistook His Wife For a Hat,* writing: 'they tell us nothing about the individual and *his* history, they convey nothing of the person, and the experience of the person, as he faces, and struggles to survive, his disease'. He notes that many descriptions of people in medical studies 'could as well apply to a rat as a human being'. I think that at the centre of being ill is hoping not just for treatment but to feel, once again, like a human being. I no longer wish to live as a rat.

*

In the *Diagnostic and Statistical Manual of Mental Disorders,* the word 'hysteria' disappeared in 1980 when the DSM III was published. No longer was 'hysterical neurosis' mentioned, as in the 1968 manual, but instead switched fully to the term 'conversion'. Yet I know that once a word disappears from a manual it does not instantly vanish from a practitioner's lips. I've heard terms outdated by decades being repeated back to me during a diagnosis. Hysteria has remained within psychiatry's consciousness (or perhaps, subconscious, when it comes to the Freudians).

And so I am not surprised when I read the World Health Organization's *ICD-10: Classification of Mental and Behavioural Disorders* and find the word 'hysteria', even if it's being used to qualify the 'conversion' classification. They write:

> The term 'hysteria' has not been used in the title for
> any disorder in Chapter V(F) of ICD-10 because
> of its many and varied shades of meaning. Instead,
> 'dissociative' has been preferred, to bring together
> disorders previously termed hysteria, of both
> dissociative and conversion types.

This was published in 2018 and I find it interesting that neither gender nor stigma are mentioned. 'Shades of meaning' is oddly neutral for an illness that is anything but. Later in the ICD, conversion is defined in starkly familiar and old-fashioned terms:

> The term 'conversion' is widely applied to some
> of these disorders, and implies that the unpleasant
> affect, engendered by the problems and conflicts that
> the individual cannot solve, is somehow transformed
> into the symptoms.

Once again, blame appears in the borders of a definition of illness. 'The individual cannot solve' echoes as I read through the long document, probably arduously formatted by WHO interns. I am being glib to soften the rage. This definition, like so much when it comes to illness, is just a guess. No one knows why this illness manifests (*somehow* transformed'), yet the individual is left to experience an 'unpleasant affect' with few answers but self-blame to hold on to.

While the word 'hysteria' is somewhat gone from medical textbooks, its aura of blame and diminishing of (mostly) women's pain remains. The word is gone but its legacy remains when women enter the waiting room. I would argue that living with this illness, which is not only nebulous but fraught with connotations, is a lot to unpack in the standard ten hours of government-supported therapy. In response, I imagine WHO, embodied only as a booming clear voice, telling me that this is simply a conflict 'that the individual cannot solve'.

*

It's hard to write about therapy because so much of the work is outside that little room with the tissue box. (One of the things I like about Dr Robert is that his tissue box is tucked away on his desk. The chair I sit in is firm; I do not sink down into it and so, for the hour I'm there, we are physically on the same level.) It's hard to write, too, because when you're in that little room, it's just you. You are the centre. There are no distractions, although I have managed to memorise every little object, each memento in that office. Your job as patient is to lay out your problems, to voice them in ways you have not before and to trust that the other person is not only listening, but hearing you with kindness.

Siri Hustvedt writes in *The Shaking Woman* that 'the

intimacy of the dialogue between analyst and patient is also rather frightening. Frankly, saying *everything* on my mind has a terrifying ring to it.' Hustvedt talks of potentially seeing a psychoanalyst, where I see a psychologist (no prescription pad for me; that is left for my GP and the psychiatrist I cannot afford). Before seeing Dr Robert, I shared her fear. I did not want to dig into this illness and as a consequence, learn about some grand failing of mine (or perhaps, depending on the psych, my parents) that has led me down this path. But Dr Robert's approach has not been metaphorical, it has been more concrete. He is not preoccupied with *why* this illness has fallen to me, but how he can help me live.

While I've been obsessed with the *why*, his approach has meant that by recounting each seizure, we have brainstormed ways for me to remove the fear associated with them. For a time, this meant that when I went to the supermarket and felt the walls around me melt and stretch out, I was to take a breath and narrate the experience as though I was outside of my own body. An impartial observer looking on at a scared animal. I created a persona, gave him the voice of David Attenborough and named him Captain FlimFlam. (It's important to have humour in these circumstances, Dr Robert will tell me more than once.) At first, the persona is shoddy and flits back into panic when I find my legs cannot move or someone looks at me askew. I wonder if I'm no good at being impartial, then question why I have chosen an old white man's voice to be the centre of rationality. But over the weeks, distractions aside, it gets a little better. I make jokes to myself and, in a state where it's hard to control the line between speaking aloud and in my head, I chuckle to myself in the supermarket aisle.

While viewing the changing colours around me, I shift between feeling terror to viewing them as a joke only I can see. On the days where I manage to feel a little more upbeat, the seizures are shorter and less severe. Dr Robert and I decide that while I have no control over when they occur or how they present, my own reaction to them will change how much effect they have. I'm surprised at how much of a difference a (mostly transitory) sense of acceptance can make. Although I shouldn't be. Studies have found that when people who experience chronic pain undergo therapy that teaches them to avoid trying to control the pain, they experience less distress. Researchers Samantha Brooks, Katharine Rimes and Trudie Chalder write that trying to control the uncontrollable can result in 'reduced physical functioning, higher pain identity and more serious perceived consequences'. The irony of giving up control and then having a better understanding and experience of one's symptoms is not lost on me. But the relief I feel at being able to move through the experience safely is astounding, even if it comes and goes.

Because the nature of my symptoms is forever changing, my life often has the sense of being uneven. I can track periods of time by illness. I remember the balmy summer months and how, when left alone, I was unable to stop myself singing aloud while walking down the street. It was such an odd symptom; I refuse to sing in front of my dearest friends for embarrassment at how off-key and stilted my voice is. *Perhaps I was a new person now, without fear of my voice being heard?* Perhaps not. The symptom drifted away, back to that mysterious place it had come from.

I remember how white washes of vision came one winter when I followed a friend to a haunted doll exhibition at a community museum an hour north of Adelaide. The flash of photographers brought on hallucinations, strange shifting washes hovering around the shape of visitors. I would later laugh with Dr Robert at how I could tell few people that I was seeing things in a haunted place, for fear they would take it the wrong way.

The evolving nature of my symptoms – coming and going like the seasons – has not been easy. Change has always triggered anxiety in me. It's not an unusual fear; psychologists R Nicholas Carleton, Donald Sharpe and Gordon Asmundson have written that fear of the unknown might 'be the most basic component of pathological anxiety' and 'a fundamental component of all anxiety disorders'. Writer HP Lovecraft, too, wrote in *Supernatural Horror in Literature* that 'the oldest and strongest emotion of mankind is fear, and the oldest and strongest kind of fear is fear of the unknown'.

While once change ruled my life on a smaller scale (a last-minute change of restaurant plans could make my breath pause), now each day is governed by change. One month to the next, I'm not sure whether I'll find my limbs paralysed or be unable to stop muttering to myself in the street. I have been forced to adapt to my body's unpredictability. Some days, I cannot leave the house because of a sense that once outside I will fall quickly and deeply into sickness. But on others I feel comforted by the thought that what I have survived before, I will survive again.

I remember when I was a child waiting at the hospital with Mum and my aunt, keeping Yiayia company during chemotherapy. Aunty Zeffie had been to the doctor in the past week and had to describe her family history. She told her doctor about her sister – my Yiayia – and her pacemaker, her skin cancer, her bowel cancer. The doctor said offhandedly, 'And when did she die?' I looked to Yiayia for her reaction to the story before I shared mine. She was laughing, her grin reaching back to show the hint of her gold filling. She was tired, lying in a hospital bed, but laughing at still being here and surrounded by her family.

My story is different from hers, much less painful. But it shares the sense of a journey, long and hard but also tinted brighter with laughter. In the first days of my illness, as I wandered near my home on afternoon walks gazing at the trees as if I had never seen one before, I could not imagine myself being here. In this place of half-acceptance. With mental illness, so often we are told to overcome. To fight those daily battles. But fighting against illness can often feel like fighting against yourself. Trying to accept it, as impossible as it is to do completely, is a relief. It feels like the sweetness of laughter at the end of the treatment.

HYSTERIA

Being ill can take a lot; in this new life, my ability to stay grounded feels all the more precarious. But here I am: still living, breathing, even singing.

EPILOGUE

When it comes it's like being torn open. I am slumped in the passenger seat, sick of being in the car after a long drive. Mathew navigates the dark roads through Santa Barbara and I can just make out the red tile of the buildings past the street lights. As the blur of oncoming traffic reaches my eyes, it happens. My vision twists and turns and I let out a breath that sounds like a groan. Mathew, still looking at the road, reaches for me. 'Are you okay?' It hurts, I tell him. I take an old towel I left in the back seat and press it to my eyes. To stop the spinning; the burning.

Mathew turns the car back the way we came, to our motel room, and I feel myself shrinking into the towel. Disappearing, almost, but with a stiffness in my limbs that doesn't seem to budge. Each block we pass: 'We're nearly there. Just a little more,' and I can hear him but I can't and my body has gone cold.

Mathew parks and he is quiet now. Later, I'll wonder if he's scared but he takes it all in his stride so much that I start to think maybe he doesn't feel the fear as I do. I hear the car door open and I will my arms to move: to lift myself out of this seat. But they don't and I realise I no longer feel the rough texture of the bleached towel against my eyelids. Mathew lifts me out; I lean on him half-slumped.

The well-lit car park and stairwell to our room make it hard to see. We have to go up the stairs but I don't know how to do it. It feels beyond my ability. The stairway is narrow and I force my hands to hold each rail so I can drag up my locked legs. My face feels slack and scared and as I approach the second step, I hear giggling. Not cruel, but uncomfortable. I look up and see two girls, late teens – visiting a college for the weekend perhaps? – waiting at the top of the stairs. They need to get down and, some-how, my own discomfort grows. I curl myself against one rail, allowing them to pass as Mathew stands behind me. Supporting me. Later, I'll ask him if he noticed the way the girls laughed and he'll be confused. 'What girls?' he'll ask.

Together, somehow, we push my body up the stairs and into the room. Mathew carries me on to the bed, as much as he can with one of my legs dragging across the old carpet. I lie there and I am just parts. Feet in shoes. Arms in jacket. And he removes the pieces of outer clothing one by one until I am left with jeans and a t-shirt and tears collecting on my jaw, dropping onto my chest. I am a child and he moves my body into position; I am a hundred years old and feel like I no longer fit. I can't bear to be seen, lying and seizing on this shining beige motel quilt. I had thought – hoped – that because it had been so long since a bad one, perhaps I had imagined all of this. That it was never this bad; just little episodes. Only *just* outside the realm of normal.

EPILOGUE

*

I crack open essayist Joan Didion's *The White Album*: 'We tell ourselves stories in order to live.' In order to live *through*, perhaps would be more accurate for me. I needed to weave a story about being sick in order to survive it. Didion continues, 'We live entirely, especially if we are writers, by the imposition of a narrative line upon disparate images, by the "ideas" with which we have learned to freeze the shifting phantasmagoria which is our actual experience.' I became sick and I wrote a book about it, and by doing so, crafted a narrative. The first onslaught of seizures now held significance despite the fact that, at the time, all I felt was withdrawn and confused. Perhaps I've shaped it into a story in the hope that I could write my way into an ending. Writer Leslie Jamison treads similar ground in *The Recovering: Intoxication and Its Aftermath*. Jamison writes, 'when it came to drinking, I'd parsed my motivations in a thousand sincere conversations – with friends, with therapists, with my mother, with my boyfriends – and all my self-understanding hadn't granted me any release from compulsion'. I recognise the pattern; I've talked to Mathew, Mum, Dad, a GP, a psychiatrist, a psychologist, a neurologist. But most of all, I've spoken to myself again and again through the page. Every time I went to write, I wrote sincerely of the truth I thought I was living. Yet still, like Jamison, I was not released from illness.

*

I wrote this book in a heady rush when the illness came. At first, I began writing for myself: to understand its fluctuations. To document what was happening to me. To be absorbed in something productive. Later, many people will try to speak around the illness. They will say they *wish* they could write so quickly and when I try to draw the fact of sickness back into the conversation, they will look sheepish. These things, I try not to learn, are better left unsaid.

But as I wrote, not only did the book change but I did too. It morphed from a coping mechanism to a desire to break the prevalent stigma of being ill. More so, to make severe mental illness something other than abject. I'm not sure that my contribution will make any change, although I wish more than anything that a little more understanding will be released into the world. But at the very least, in writing it and delivering it to the hands of Mum and Mathew, *Hysteria* allowed me to share what was happening in my mind while the seizures shut off my ability to speak or move. This let them see me within my ill body, still very much myself, yet intrinsically altered.

I read a study (I'm only just learning to stop searching for answers) where, after talking to the chronically ill and their families, therapist Peggy Penn writes that, 'the experience of the illness produces incrementally traumatising experiences, not only for the person with the illness, but also for other members of the family'. It hurts to realise my illness could have affected my family in such a way. I realise that as I became sicker, I stopped talking and wrote more. Like Kaethe Weingarten, a psychologist who receives an aggressive cancer diagnosis, I 'lived in silence: certain that no one could bear to hear the feelings and thoughts I had following my year of treatment'. Mathew tells me I stop talking about being ill months after the book is complete. It takes his words for me to realise this: I don't want to be the person talking *over* and *over* about their illness to their family. Instead, I write.

For some, this will improve their symptoms, as found in a 1999 study of people with asthma or rheumatoid arthritis. Talk therapy, too, of which writing detailed accounts of illness plays a part, has long been thought of as psychology's magic cure. But for me, despite the book I have created, I remain sick. Yet I don't think of writing as a failed cure; it has been a lifeline. Like a telephone wire, it runs between me and the outside world.

And writing *Hysteria* has not only connected me with my family but the other women who experienced seizures – labelled hysterical or otherwise. I found them all by accident, stumbled across through obsessive reading, but with each of them I felt an unexplained connection. Edith, Mary, Katharina, Blanche. They are from different times and share privileges that many other women who experienced illness were not afforded either because of their race, wealth, sexuality or family support. I often think of the women who've struggled with this who haven't been let into history books or medical studies. When I think of the other bodies affected, I cannot help but think of my own privilege as a white woman with a middle-class family. I lived through this mostly because of my family, who have booked psychiatrist appointments and driven me to the hospital for testing. Who have listened and stayed. But perhaps most of all, who have read my words about what it means to be sick.

*

I find an astrology column on the street. It's glued down to the bitumen by the wet of the rain. There is one sign: Libra. My sign. Someone has torn around the edges gently. I wonder if they placed it on the street for me to find. Or perhaps they wanted to keep it with them and when reaching into their pocket, it had flown away with the wind. The column tells me that soon, I will experience the fleeting gift of wisdom. I don't think it knows I have written hundreds of pages about the pain of not knowing. Wisdom feels elusive.

How can I ever show what this is like? I deal in words; they feel hollow next to breathing walls and flickering lights. How can chronic illness be fully described, when an essay or a book always ends? Writer Kazuo Ishiguro said in his Nobel acceptance speech, 'stories are about one person saying to another: This is the way it feels to me. Can you understand what I'm saying? Does it also feel this way to you?'

*

After living this way for the past two years, I've learnt that illness interrupts life. Yes, this is inevitable. But I've found it's also true that life interrupts illness. I go outside. Live, little by little. I'm aware that these small bursts wouldn't mean much to most, but to me they feel like a deep gasp after minutes spent underneath the water's surface. I live and am caught up in the act of making a meal for Mathew – a complicated one, with two courses. I cut the vegetables sitting at the kitchen table, my body unable to hold itself upright for long periods as it once did. But even with this change, the thrill of creating is not dampened. I lose myself in a moment where my dog settles her chin on my thigh, falling comfortably into sleep. I watch her breath push its way through her grey whiskers. I visit the library more than I ever have. I read feverishly; nothing that could be classified as medical but stories about an octopus, a war, a paper house.

I keep working, shaving down my schedule as much as I can afford. The work makes me sicker, as work does for most of us living with a chronic illness, but I seize and breathe through it. I know I will come out okay, just a little shaken.

And somewhere in the next year, I find myself forgetting. Not all the time. It's a dangerous thing to forget in a moment of strength and be ill for the next week. But it doesn't hurt as much, most days. Sometimes I am hit with the ache of a life lost when I see a job posting that I'd love but could not do. In one way, my career will never be what it once could have been. Yet now I see this as a good thing.

Perhaps I've stumbled into something better. The ache hits harder when I see a parent pointing out aeroplanes to a little one tottering beside them. I never dreamt of children or marriage when I was a child myself. And as an adult, it has barely crossed my mind. I was transfixed by animals, books, B-grade horror. Children seemed like something far off that I needn't even consider. But now, it hurts to know that with this iteration of illness, some things might no longer be available to me.

Weeks ago, I had a coffee with an old friend. She has beautiful deep-set eyes and a gentle laugh. We sat together for hours over our coffee and we shared what we wanted out of life. After such a long time apart, I was too scared to tell her how limited my body has become and instead spoke only of desire. She smiled at me after I finished talking: 'Katerina, you have time.' I try to repeat her words to myself in these moments when I think of loss. I have time. Time to enjoy another life, a little different from the one I'd constructed in my mind.

FURTHER READING

EDITH

American Psychiatric Association, *Diagnostic and Statistical Manual of Mental Disorders* (1st ed.), Washington, 1952.

American Psychiatric Association, *Diagnostic and Statistical Manual of Mental Disorders* (2nd ed.), Washington, 1968.

American Psychiatric Association, *Diagnostic and Statistical Manual of Mental Disorders* (4th ed.), Washington, 1994.

American Psychiatric Association, *Diagnostic and Statistical Manual of Mental Disorders* (5th ed.), Washington, 2013.

Amiel, HF, *The Journal Intime*, MacMillan, New York, 1882.

Aviv, R, 'How a Young Woman Lost Her Identity', *New Yorker*, 2019, <www.newyorker.com/magazine/2018/04/02/how-a-young-woman-lost-her-identity>.

Department of Health, 'Prevalence of Mental Disorders in the Australian Population', 2009, <www1.health.gov.au/internet/publications/publishing.nsf/Content/mental-pubs-m-mhaust2-toc~mental-pubs-m-mhaust2-hig~mental-pubs-m-mhaust2-hig-pre>.

Hoffman, FJ, *The Twenties: American Writing in American Life and Letters*, Viking, New York, 1955.

Jacobson, E, 'Depersonalization', *Journal of the American Psychoanalytic Association*, vol. 7, no. 4, 1959, 581–610.

Jacobson, E, 'Observations on the Psychological Effects of Imprisonment on Female Political Prisoners', in KR Eissler (ed.), *Searchlights on Delinquency*, International Universities Press, New York, 1949.

Rice, X, 'The Cellist of Auschwitz', *New Statesman*, 2015, <www.newstatesman.com/world/europe/2015/10/cellist-auschwitz>.

Ricke, LA, *Psy Fi: Nazi Psychoanalysis*, University of Minnesota Press, Minneapolis, 2002.

Russell, D (writer/director), *Silver Linings Playbook*, The Weinstein Company, 2012.

Sartre, J-P, *Nausea*, Penguin Books, London, 2000.

Schilder, P, *Medical Psychology, International Universities Press*, New York, 1953.

Schröter, M, Mühlleitner, E & Ulrike, M, 'Edith Jacobson: Forty Years in Germany (1897–1938)', *The Annual of Psychoanalysis*, vol. 32, 2004, 199–215.

Simeon, D & Abugel, J, *Feeling Unreal: Depersonalization Disorder and the Loss of the Self*, Oxford University Press, Oxford, 2008.

Sontag, S, *Illness as Metaphor*, Penguin Books, London, 2009.

MARY

Almond, PC, *Demonic Possession and Exorcism in Early Modern England*, Cambridge University Press, Cambridge, 2009.

Appignanesi, L, *Mad, Bad and Sad: A History of Women and the Mind Doctors from 1800 to the Present*, Virago, London, 2009.

Bratfos, O, 'Organic versus Non-Organic Diseases: A Distinction Necessary for Rational Practice', *Tidsskr Nor Laegeforen*, vol. 110, no. 7, 1990, 865–868.

Ding, JM & Kanaan, RAA, 'Conversion Disorder: A Systematic Review of Current Terminology', *General Hospital Psychiatry*, vol. 45, 2017, 51–55.

Harré, HR, 'Mind-Body Dualism', *International Encyclopedia of the Social & Behavioral Sciences*, Elsevier, New York, 2001, 9885–9889.

Hustvedt, S, *The Shaking Woman or A History of My Nerves*, Hodder & Stoughton, London, 2010.

Janet, P, *The Major Symptoms of Hysteria: Fifteen Lectures Given in the Medical School of Harvard University*, Macmillan, New York, 1907.

Jorden, E, *A Briefe Discourse of a Disease Called the Suffocation of the Mother*, printed by John Windet, 1603, <www.historyofemotions.org.au/media/92110/A_briefe_discourse_of_a_disease_called_t.pdf>.

MacDonald, M, *Witchcraft and Hysteria in Elizabethan London: Edward Jorden and the Mary Glover Case*, Routledge, London, 1991.

Micale, MS, 'Hysteria and Its Historiography: A Review of Past and Present Writings', *History of Science*, vol. 27, no. 3, 1989, 223–261.

Micale, MS, 'On the "Disappearance" of Hysteria: A Study in the Clinical Deconstruction of a Diagnosis', *Isis*, vol. 84, no. 3, 1993, 496–526.

Micklem, N, *The Nature of Hysteria*, Routledge, London, 2017.

North, CS, 'The Classification of Hysteria and Related Disorders: Historical and Phenomenological Considerations', *Behavioral Sciences*, vol. 5, no. 4, 2015, 496–517.

Orr-Andrawes, A, 'The Case of Anna O.: A Neuropsychiatric Perspective', *Journal of the American Psychoanalytic Association*, vol. 35, 1987, 387–419.

Pavon, G &Vaes, J, 'Bio-Genetic vs. Psycho-Environmental Conceptions of Schizophrenia and their Role in Perceiving Patients in Human Terms', *Psychosis*, vol. 9, no. 3, 2017, 245–253.

Raese, J, 'The Pernicious Effect of Mind/Body Dualism in Psychiatry', *Journal of Psychiatry*, vol. 18, no. 1, 2015, 219–226.

Tasca, C, Rapetti, M & Carta, MG, 'Women and Hysteria in the History of Mental Health', *Clinical Practice & Epidemiology in Mental Health*, vol. 8, 2012, 110–119.

Taylor, C, *Dying: A Memoir*, Text, Melbourne, 2016.

Thien, M, *Dogs at the Perimeter*, Granta, London, 2011.

Woolf, V, *Orlando*, Wordsworth, London, 1995.

KATHARINA

Atkinson, M, *Traumata*, University of Queensland Press, Queensland, 2018.

Beauchard, D, *Epileptic*, Jonathan Cape, London, 2005.

Breuer, J & Freud, S, *Studies on Hysteria*, Basic Books, USA, 2000.

Cixous, H, 'The Laugh of the Medusa', *Signs*, vol. 1, no. 4, 1976, 875–893.

Herman, J, *Trauma & Recovery: The Aftermath of Violence – From Domestic Abuse to Political Terror*, Basic Books, New York, 2015.

Hungerford, Jocelyn, 'Women Who Write About Their Feelings and Lives', *Sydney Review of Books*, 2019, <sydneyreviewofbooks.com/atkinson-traumata-lilley-oysters-get-bored/>.

Hustvedt, Siri, *The Shaking Woman or A History of My Nerves*, Hodder & Stoughton, London, 2010.

Ireland, J, 'A Speculum in the Text: Freud's "Katharina" and Maupassant's "Le Signe",' *MLN*, vol. 113, no. 5, 1998, 1089–1110.

Janet, P, *The Major Symptoms of Hysteria: Fifteen Lectures Given in the Medical School of Harvard University*, Macmillan, New York, 1907.

Kaplan, M, 'Bertha Pappenheim', *Jewish Women's Archive*, 2011, <jwa.org/encyclopedia/article/pappenheim-bertha>.

Lempert, T & Schmidt, D, 'Natural History and Outcome of Psychogenic Seizures: A Clinical Study in 50 Patients', *Journal of Neurology*, vol. 237, no. 1, 1990, 35–38.

Lesser, RP, 'Treatment and Outcome of Psychogenic Nonepileptic Seizures', *Epilepsy Currents*, vol. 3, no. 6, 2003, 198–200.

O'Sullivan, S, *It's All in Your Head: True Stories of Imaginary Illness*, Chatto & Windus, London, 2015.

Prior, S, 'Sian Prior on Curing Shyness and Finding Enoughness', *Dumbo Feather*, 2017, <www.dumbofeather.com/articles/how-to-cure-shyness/>.

Prior, S, *Shy: A Memoir*, Text, Melbourne, 2014.

Woolf, V, *Mrs Dalloway*, Wordsworth, London, 1996.

BLANCHE

Benjamin, M, 'The Disordered Self: Philosophy, Memoir and Madness', in
    G Araoz, F Alves & K Jaworski (eds), *Rethinking Madness:*
    Interdisciplinary and Multicultural Reflections, Brill, Leiden, 2013.

Claretie, J, *Les Amours d'un Interne*, Hachette Livre, Paris, 2012.

Collings, A, 'Discovering the Lost Photos of a Psychiatric Hospital', *VICE*,
    2015, <www.vice.com/en_au/article/exq7vw/discovering-lost-photos-
    of-prestwichs-psychiatric-patients-115>.

Didi-Huberman, G, 'The Figurative Incarnation of the Sentence (Notes on
    the "Autographic" Skin)', *Cabinet*, vol. 13, 2004.

Hustvedt, A, *Medical Muses: Hysteria in Nineteenth-Century Paris*,
    Bloomsbury, London, 2011.

KATERINA

Alter, A, 'John Green Tells a Story of Emotional Pain and Crippling Anxiety.
    His Own', *New York Times*, 2017, <www.nytimes.com/2017/10/10/
    books/john-green-anxiety-obsessive-compulsive-disorder.html>.

American Psychiatric Association, *Diagnostic and Statistical Manual of Mental*
    Disorders (2nd ed.), Washington, 1968.

American Psychiatric Association, *Diagnostic and Statistical Manual of Mental*
    Disorders (3rd ed.), Washington, 1980.

Brooks, S, Rimes, K & Chalder, T, 'The Role of Acceptance in Chronic
    Fatigue Syndrome', *Journal of Psychosomatic Research*, vol. 71, no. 6,
    2011, 411–415.

Carleton, RN, Sharpe, D & Asmundson, GJG, 'Anxiety Sensitivity and
    Intolerance of Uncertainty: Requisites of the Fundamental Fears?',
    Behavior Research & Therapy, vol. 45, 2007, 2307–2316.

Castle, W (director), *House on Haunted Hill*, William Castle Productions,
    1959.

Chiccehitto Hindman, J, *Sounds Like Titanic: A Memoir*, W. W. Norton
    Company, New York, 2019.

Cixous, H, *Stigmata: Escaping Texts*, Routledge, London, 1998.

Docker, K & Smith, A (directors), *You Can't Ask That*, ABC TV, 2018.

Friedmann, J, *Things That Helped: Essays*, Scribe Publications, Melbourne,
    2017.

Hustvedt, S, *The Shaking Woman or A History of My Nerves*, Hodder &
    Stoughton, London, 2010.

FURTHER READING

Kofman, L, *Imperfect*, Affirm Press, Melbourne, 2019.

Lovecraft, HP, *Supernatural Horror in Literature*, Wermod & Wermod Publishing, UK, 2013.

Myers, L, *Psychogenic Non-Epileptic Seizures: A Guide*, CreateSpace Independent Publishing, South Carolina, 2014.

Proust, M, *In Search of Lost Time*, Penguin Books, London, 2003.

Sacks, Oliver, *The Man Who Mistook His Wife for a Hat*, Picador, London, 1986.

Sontag, S, *Illness as Metaphor*, Penguin Books, London, 2009.

World Health Organization, *The ICD-10 Classification of Mental and Behavioural Disorders: Clinical Descriptions and Diagnostic Guidelines*, Geneva, 1992.

Wright, F, 'This Woman Is Hysterical', *Meanjin*, vol. 78, no. 2, 2019, 54–64.

EPILOGUE

Didion, J, *The White Album*, Macmillan, New York, 1990.

Ishiguro, K, *My Twentieth Century Evening – and Other Small Breakthroughs*, Knopf, New York, 2017.

Jamison, L, *The Recovering: Intoxication and Its Aftermath*, Granta, London, 2018.

Penn, P, 'Chronic Illness: Trauma, Language, and Writing: Breaking the Silence', *Family Process*, vol. 40, no. 1, 2001, 33–52.

Smyth, JM, 'Effects of Writing about Stressful Experiences on Symptom Reduction in Patients with Asthma or Rheumatoid Arthritis', *JAMA*, vol. 281, 1999, 1304–1309.

ACKNOWLEDGMENTS

As a reader, I always turn to the acknowledgments first to read the warmth of the thank yous. It feels somewhat wondrous to be writing this myself.

I would like to acknowledge that this book was written on the traditional lands of the Kaurna people. I am an uninvited guest who lives and works on stolen, unceded land. I pay my respects to Elders past and present.

To my family – Mathew, Mum, Dad – not only are you my first readers but the people I most want to impress. Thank you for your support and care.

My dear friends who have listened to me throughout this process and my illness. Thank you to Annie Robinson, Melody Wong, Aimee Knight and Emily Palmer.

I've been deeply grateful to have connected with a publisher who not only understands what I hope to do, but puts so much into improving the work. Thank you, Harriet McInerney. This experience has been so much greater for having you in it. And thank you to managing editor Paul O'Beirne for his enthusiasm and oversight along the

ACKNOWLEDGMENTS

way. I'm also sincerely grateful for Alissa Dinallo's beautiful cover design.

Thank you to my agent Sarah McKenzie for her kind words and championing this book throughout its journey to publication.

And a warm thanks to copy-editor Jocelyn Hungerford, who challenged me to consider trauma in a new light and who took the utmost care in sharpening my sentences.

The 'Katharina' chapter was written at Varuna, The Writers' House on a fellowship awarded by Writers SA. Thank you to Sarah Tooth, the Writers SA team, Veechi, Amy, Vera, Sheila and the fellow writers – Barry, Dias, Viv, Madeline, Zoya – I shared that incredible week with.

Parts of the 'Blanche' chapter first appeared in an essay for *Meanjin* titled 'What Is Illness/Where Is Illness'. Thank you, Tess Smurthwaite, for your enthusiasm.

A last thank you to the women and non-binary people who came before me and who continue to work to build understanding and compassion for people living with severe mental illness. I feel privileged to share this space with you.